PLACE NAMES KEYED TO
CHAPTER NUMBERS

2 London
3 Sherwood Forest
5 Tinsley Green
6 Greenwich
7 Lisbon
8,10 Barcelona
9 La Mancha
11 Gomera (Canary Is.)
12 Wierum
13 Baarle
14 Namur
15 Waterloo
16 Echternach
17 Arles-sur-Tech
18 Oradour-sur-Glane
19 Hauterives
20,21 Paris
22 Y
23 Hackenberg
24 Port Grimaud
25 Berne
27-37 Rome
38 Gurro
39 Bologna
40 Grazzano Visconti
41 Savona
42 Ravenna
43 Genoa
44 Collodi
45 Viterbo
46 Verona
47 Campiglia Marittima
1,48 Florence
49 Marostica
50 Messina
51 Bagheria
52 Hamelin
53 Munich
54 Heidelberg
55 Gergweis
56 Ruhpolding
57 Nuremberg
58 Bayreuth
59 Bremen
60 Starnberg
61 Plech ("Kansas City")
62 Nieder-Beerbach
63 Vienna
64 Neusiedler See
65 Murau
66 Oberndorf
67 Klein Walsertal
68 Lidice
69 Wieliczka
70 Budapest
71 Gaina
72 Postumia
73 Belgrade
74 Monoklissia
75 Mount Athos
76 Langada
77-79 Moscow

© HAMMOND INCORPORATED, Maplewood, N.J.

BALTIC SEA

U. S. S. R.

Moscow
77-79 ★

Warsaw ★
P O L A N D

Crakow
●●● 69

Prague
ECHOSLOVAKIA

enna ★ 63
● 64
ourg
I A
5

Budapest
★ 70
H U N G A R Y

71 ● RUMANIA

72 ● Zagreb

73 ★
Belgrade

Y U G O S L A V I A

Bucharest ★

B U L G A R I A

, 48

ALBANIA

74 ●
76 ●
● 75

T U R K E Y

G R E E C E

50 ●

51
Sicily

Athens ★

S E A

MALTA

EUROPEAN DETOURS

A Travel Guide to Unusual Sights

NE SPERNAS DIGITI QVO DEXTERA COELI
SO NVMQVAM VISOS MORTALIBVS ORBES
VIT PARVO FRAGILIS MOLIMINE VITRI
FACINVS CVI NON TITANIA QVONDAM
PVBES CONGESTIS MONTIBVS ALTIS
AM SVPERAS CONATA ASCENDERE IN A

THOMAS PERELL

GALILEO'S FINGER

EUROPEAN
DETOURS

A Travel Guide to
Unusual Sights

BY NINO LO BELLO

A GINIGER BOOK
published in association with

INCORPORATED
MAPLEWOOD, NEW JERSEY 07040

Library of Congress Cataloging in Publication Data

Lo Bello, Nino.
    European detours.

    "A Giniger book."
    1. Europe—Description and travel—1971-   —Guide-
books.   I. Title.
D909.L6   1981   914'.04558   80-19901
ISBN 0-8437-3375-6

First Edition

Designer: Ernst Reichl

To Christopher Columbus,
history's greatest traveler, and
to Marco Polo,
history's greatest tourist.
From their Italian heritage,
I may have derived a wanderlust and
curiosity of my own . . .

CONTENTS

EUROPEAN DETOURS

A Travel Guide to Unusual Sights

(Unless otherwise indicated, all photographs are by the author.)

BY WAY OF INTRODUCTION

THIS BOOK does not fall into any category. It is a travel book that is not a travel book in the ordinary sense. Though it is a treasury of travel information, it won't tell you how to get there and it won't tell you the practical things other travel guides provide. In these pages I have sought to report on the not-to-be-believed sites and sights of Europe, which you will enjoy for themselves and even enjoy getting to, seeing areas and meeting people you never would have come across.

Partly because I nourish a touristic tapeworm and partly because Europe may have already become old hat for the tourist, I have spent well over a decade and a half on a hunt for unusual attractions, places hardly ever mentioned in the fine print of your guidebook's footnotes. By not shackling myself with the handcuffs of a timetable and by nosing into obscure corners of Europe to bring to light these truffles of information, I have probably logged upwards of 448,660 tourist miles. This is equivalent to about a zillion hours of fun.

During more than fifteen years of eye-browsing on these treasure hunts, I have amassed a rubberneck's collection of curiosa—the unusual, the fantastic, the unparalleled, the obscure, the weird, the incredible, the unique— most of which are usually overlooked by the time-strapped tourist who, to accumulate fodder for his brag and baggage, is always, it seems to me, very busy going somewhere else. Yes, the accent is on the strange. And what's wrong with that?

The bug that bit me and infused me with this hang-up for oddball tourist attractions was Galileo's finger. That was back in 1956, shortly after the Hungarian revolution. Once the block-busting story in Budapest fizzled out, I hied myself back to Rome, and it was then I first heard about Galileo and his finger. The tip came from an usher at the Rome Opera House, my dear friend Luigi Gasperini, who said that, when the great Italian astronomer died in 1642, somebody cut off several fingers of his right hand. One of the fingers was on display, he remembered, either in Pisa or Florence.

"Think of it," said Gasperini, drawing a deep breath, "the finger that belonged to the hand that belonged to the body that had the brain that conceived those great experiments in physics and astronomy over three centuries ago!"

The thought somehow fascinated. Galileo's finger indeed! But putting a finger on what is probably the least known tourist sight in Italy was no snap. An initial inquiry was made at Italy's National Tourist Office in Rome. The man in charge behaved as if the quest were the figment of an unhinged mind.

"The finger of Galileo?" he muttered, his hoax-proof radar painfully on the alert. "*Ammazza!* Where did you get such a fantastic idea?" Nevertheless, he summoned a trio of colleagues who, upon being told of Galileo's finger, collectively shook their heads and discreetly maintained straight faces.

My next stop was Pisa, where Galileo had taught at the famed university and where he had propped himself out of the Leaning Tower to drop objects of different weights in order to prove that they would fall with the same speed. When apprised of Galileo's missing digit, several of the city officials screwed up their faces in bureaucratic skepticism.

The scent of the finger seemed to grow dimmer and dimmer on my way to Florence. But now Lady Luck beckoned a finger of her own. At the Church of Santa Croce, where Galileo is buried and where also rest the bones of Michelangelo and Machiavelli, the attendant replied: "Yes, I know the finger. Funny, you're the second person in ten years who's asked about it. Last I heard, it was in the National Library. Try there."

The Library people said they had had the finger for many years but did not quite know what to do with it. So they gave it to the Museum of the History of Science at the side of the Arno River. At the Museum, located at Piazza de' Giudici 1, a custodian with a hacking cough sold me a ticket for two hundred lire, made me sign the tourist register, and sent me upstairs one flight to Room Number 6, crammed with many of Galileo's personal possessions (a lens, a compass, two telescopes, thermometers, a chair and four wooden bedlegs).

At last, after the musty labyrinth of crammed exhibits, I came upon the finger, Galileo's finger, the middle finger from his right hand. There it was in a showcase on an eye-high shelf, enclosed in an egg-shaped, gold-decorated glass container placed atop a piece of marble, cylindrical in shape, on which a Latin sentence by Thomas Perellius, an astronomer of the University of Pisa, had been inscribed. The finger is pointing skyward, toward the solar system as Galileo interpreted it, which, because it had not been in harmony with certain passages of the Scrip-

tures, had brought on his trial before the Inquisition and forced him to abstain from Copernican heresy.

From an office attendant, one Fabio Fabiani, I learned that on March 12, 1737, when Galileo's body was being moved from a tiny room in the belltower next to the Chapel of Saints Cosimo and Damiano for final burial in the Church of Santa Croce, Anton Francesco Gori (a nobleman who was a fanatic admirer of Galileo) cut off three of the rebel astronomer's fingers to keep as relics. Two of these fingers are in the private possession today of Dr. Luigi Rosselli Del Turco, while the right middle finger is in the Museum.

Mesmerized by Galileo's withered phalanx, indeed a curiosity that both amused and amazed me, I had now tasted the nectar of a novelty. And I wanted more. So the hunt began. And it has been going on keenly since then. The "trophies" are on the following pages. In microcosm rather than macrocosm, they add a fourth dimension to travel that I want to share with you.

If you are an armchair traveler, this mosaic of rarities may turn out to be a closetful of surprises for you. If, however, you have a thirst for discovery and your wanderlust has become a wonderlust, then this compilation of some of the most extraordinary nonesuches of Europe can provide you with the kind of fascinating travel experience you may never have had, no matter how much you may have traveled.

To make this compendium possible, there are hundreds, nay thousands, of people who helped me gather the facts. Even a list of their names would be far too long for inclusion here. Especially do I want to mention, however, the names of those people who have contributed their help and encouragement: Charles De Mangin, Jimmy Bedford, Carl Clemens, Bertha Smyth, Emilie Rooney, Anny Paulick, Luigi Gasperini, Joe Wechsberg, Alan Levy, Robert Sage, Jennings Parrott, Tom Lucey, Jim Shaw, Sonja Hansen Jacywics, Theodore Shabad, Milo Farneti, Tanya Givens Riley and my brother, John "Jit" Lo Bello, who first infected me with the travel virus.

Lastly, a special word of recognition should go to my constant travel partner, editor, wife, friend: Irene Rooney Lo Bello. She helped me scour the most remote pigeonholes of Europe, and as my alert navigator, chief of staff and radar-eyed reader of maps, always managed to guide our trusty Volkswagen to the precise target.

NINO LO BELLO
Vienna

SOME LONDON QUIRKS

IT LOOKS like any other house on the block. But wait! Nobody ever comes out of No. 23 Leinster Gardens. There is neither a doorbell nor a letter box. From the windows, no one at all peers out. And nary a soul ever sits on one of the balconies.

Thousands of people pass the strange house every day—and, in the last six decades or so, it's estimated that more than a million people have walked by and never noticed the one thing that makes it one of London's most wacky tourist attractions. Simply put, No. 23 Leinster Gardens, in the Bayswater section of London, is "The House That Never Was."

Yes, No. 23 is a sham. It's a dummy house whose door and windows are merely painted on a cement wall. Behind this deceiving facade, there is nothing except a network of girders, some train tracks and the entrance to a tunnel. Every so often a fresh coat of paint is applied to the facing wall to keep it looking like the neighboring buildings.

"The House That Never Was" was put up by London's Metropolitan Railway (the so-called "Underground" or "Tube") whose officials decided it would be the best way to hide the entrance to the subway tunnel and fill the gap in the row of houses so as not to spoil the harmonious look of the street.

London's Underground is also responsible for another quirk. Very few of the thousands of people who use the Sloane Square Underground station every day—tourists and Londoners alike—have even the faintest idea that a real river flows over their heads through a huge, prominent iron pipe that runs above the track and platform. During the war, several bombs did heavy damage to the station, but the big conduit fifteen feet overhead did not even spring a leak.

The river is the Westbourne River and it eventually flows into the Thames near the Chelsea Bridge. When London's subway system was being built over a hundred years ago, the architect's problem was that the river had to cross the train track at Sloane Square one way or another. He decided to channel the flow of water into a sturdy iron conduit and erect it overhead, making the subway station the only one in the whole world that has a river running over it. Some Londoners, however, prefer to put it the other way around: the Westbourne River is the only river in the world that runs over a Tube station.

Whichever way you put it, London still wins first honors when it comes to municipal oddities that, charmingly, go over and above the usual tourist magnets that everybody knows about. "Matey, fings ain't wot they seem to be in this here town," is the way one corner newspaper vendor puts it. He was referring to the fact that London has enough screwball surprises to give your camera a feast.

For instance: In the Windsor Town Hall, Sir Christopher Wren designed a ceiling supported by pillars. When the city fathers inspected the finished building, they didn't think the ceiling would hold up and ordered him to put in some more pillars. Well, England's greatest architect didn't think the ceiling

Number 23 Leinster Gardens in London is "The House That Never Was."

needed any more support, so he pulled a fast one. He added two "pillars" that do not do anything—they don't even reach the ceiling. The optical illusion fooled the municipal authorities and today the two sham pillars offer many a tourist amusement.

London's only perpetual lamp is on Carting Lane and is lit around the clock, burning sewer gases from below the ground. More important, it has the function of creating a current of air that sucks up gases and helps disperse them into the atmosphere, thereby eliminating the possibility of an underground explosion. All similar lamps of the past have long since disappeared and this one is truly a curiosity.

London has two of the strangest pubs in England: The first, along a street called Queen Anne's Gate, at No. 9, is a basement pub that rigidly maintains the country's strict liquor-serving hours, yet does not serve any kind of alcoholic drinks. The second, the Boot & Flogger on Southwark Street, is a pub without a license but which has the right to serve liquor beyond the legal hours otherwise in rigorous effect all over England. This unusual privilege dates back to 1364 when King Edward III, finding himself without a coin in his pocket, borrowed money from the owner of the pub. Instead of repaying the debt, he decreed for the Boot & Flogger the right to sell spirits without a license and beyond closing hours.

Indeed, London has a variety of city-osyncracies.

WHERE ROBIN HOOD IS ALIVE AND WELL

YE OLDE SHERWOOD FOREST was the house of Britain's favorite outlaw, who robbed the rich (they say) to give to the poor. For over six hundred years they have been singing songs and telling stories about Robin Hood, but no one ever gives a plug to Sherwood Forest so that tourists can visit the haunts of Robin and his Merry Men.

Sherwood Forest is a Yes-Yes. Just come and look for yourself. There is really no need to "convert" Sherwood Forest for tourism because it is all here sans benefit of commercialization. Robin Hood is alive and well today in yon green glade among the oak trees that knew the daring forest bandit intimately.

In Robin Hood's day, Sherwood Forest covered more than 100,000 acres—most of the center of the County of Nottingham. Though thousands of

Statue of Robin Hood
(with arrow missing)
in front of the wall of Nottingham Castle
(PHOTO BY IRENE ROONEY LO BELLO).

the trees were felled to build ships for England's navy in Tudor times, Sherwood is still a wooded sanctuary where a person can get lost while paying a call on Robin's haunts. Follow any one of several paths through the forest, for they all eventually meet in the village of Edwinstowe. Inside the spired church of this picturesque English hamlet, Robin and Maid Marian are said to have been married. Near Edwinstowe is a tree as old as Robin himself, the magnificent great oak tree under which the rapscallion archers loved to hold jolly court and count their booty. Today, the tree needs a bit of help with iron-plate patches to cover its wounds and chains to hold up some of the ancient branches that have become too heavy.

Robin Hood's Well is by the side of the Great North Road, halfway between the tiny towns of Doncaster and Ferrybridge. Another tourist spot is the grave of Robin Hood on the edge of Kirklees, where the colorful land pirate is said to have been buried at the age of eighty-seven. At Papplewick is the stable where Robin kept his horse and, near Ollerton, you can follow the River Moun which flowed under the footbridge that Robin and Little John used for their first encounter. Along the banks of this tiny waterway, you will find Robin Hood's cave. When you reach Whitby, the locals will tell you the story of how the legendary cad used to go there many mornings with Friar Tuck and Will Scarlet to climb to the top of the abbey's church tower and look over the surrounding countryside to see whether the Sheriff of Nottingham and his horse soldiers were undertaking one of their searches. It is also said that Robin often tested his archery skill from this tower. Serving as a favorite target for all tourist cameras, the statue of Robin Hood stands beside the wall of Nottingham Castle. Pity, but some people actually get the bright notion at times to filch Robin's arrow or both the bow and arrow as a souvenir, and it costs Nottingham about seventy dollars each time to put in a replacement.

Once a year, at the end of June, Nottingham stages its Robin Hood Day festival. Performers dressed up as Robin Hood and the Merry Men enact some of the famous exploits that allegedly took place between the years 1310 and 1360. Highlighted by Friar Tuck's jovial shenanigans, the festival also includes archery and crossbow performances, a mock battle by the Nottinghamshire and Derbyshire Veteran Arms Society, Little John's capture by the Sheriff and his spectacular rescue. Stores in Robin Hood's "home town" also sell souvenir statuettes mounted on real Sherwood oak.

The one person who does not and will not attend the festival is the Sheriff of Nottingham, an honorary political job currently held by one C. W. Judge. Mr. Judge refuses to have anything to do with the Robin Hood show because he does not think it is right to make a hero out of a crook and kidnaper. "He was nothing but a thug," asserts the current Sheriff of Nottingham. "This hero worship of a bold, bad man who did not hesitate to discharge lethal weapons at law-enforcement agents shows little regard for the fact that what he did is contrary to the laws, principles and public policy of Britain."

Sheriff Judge is quick to point out that if Robin Hood were alive today and convicted of all the crimes that have been attributed to him "in song and story," he would have to pay fines ranging up to three million dollars and face at least 475 years in prison.

9

THE ENGLISH SIGNERY

YES, CHRISTMAS PIE, the name of this town in Surrey, is enough to write home about. But then England is full of such places with queer names that titillate thousands of travelers each year. What tourist can resist making a photomontage of the towns of Ham and Sandwich which are within hiking distance of each other in Kent?

Some people travel to this country to enjoy the English scenery—and others to enjoy the English signery. There is doubtless no other country whose town and village names provide such merriment and targets for so much picture-shooting. The more "out" the name, the more likely is a visitor to whip out his camera and photograph the signpost

England is full of places with odd names, calories for your camera
(PHOTO BY IRENE ROONEY LO BELLO).

for conversation back home later on. It almost seems that every county in England vies with all the others to outdo each other in the originality of their town names. Witness such oddball monikers as the town of Whip-ma Whop-ma, or Cow Tail, or Light A Pipe, or Over Wallop, or Middle Wallop.

Many of England's town names, which have their roots and meanings in the glorious past, are indeed amusing to modern eyes and ears. So today a few of these places have become the subject of

10

daily jokes or gags. Perhaps the most punned-about town is Honeybottom but not far behind in the wit parade are such places as Pity-Me, Out of Sight, Seldom Seen, Drinkers End, and Come To Good. The last town even advertises itself before you reach it with a sign that reads: "Come To Good, 1 Mile."

One doesn't even have to travel across the map to find such places for a snappy snapshot. If you are spending a holiday in Kent, you can, by covering a distance of some fifteen miles, come across names like Daniel's Water, Loose, Snailwood, Blindgrooms, Frogs, Priestland, Rat's Castle, Rumwood and Great Love.

Several eager tourist-camerabugs have even gone in for names that are seemingly connected to each other. With a little patience that goes a long way, you can capture on film a number of "number" locations, starting with Onecote and following up with Two Bridges, Three Bridges, Four Oaks, Five Mile House, Six Bells, Seven Kings, Eight Ash Green, Nine Mile Point, Tennyson (hmmm, that would be stretching a point, wouldn't it?), Eleven Lane Ends, Twelve Heads, Forty Hill and Hundred End.

Using some imagination, an alert photo fan can make up his own category and hunt down hamlets that fit. For example, if he wanted to make a classification of unsavory names, he would have plenty of fun visiting such "unsavory" stops as Sewers End, Mudsea, Ugley, Poverty-Hole, Helion Bumpstead, Crimes, Swine, and No Man's Land—places whose charms give lie to their names in all cases.

How about handles with an aristocratic ring to them as a grouping? One could run wild with Keinton Mandeville, Ryme Intrinsica, Broadwoodwidger, Quaditchmoor, Inwardleigh, Buckland Filleigh, Sixpenny Handley, Wenden's Ambo, Tolleshunt D'Arcy, Heavering-Atte-Bower, Chignal-Smealy, Okeford Fitzpaine, Toller Porocorum, Shaugh Prior, St. Just in Roseland, Mawgan-in-Meneage, Mappowder-with-Plush, Barrow-in-Furness and Land of Nod. The last one is a name whose origin excites. One wonders just why and how it all came about. Same goes for the towns of Black Boy, Boldslaves, Great Snoring, Small Gains, Labour-in-Vain, Loose and Black Dunghill. No doubt they each have fascinating histories.

One town that raises considerable curiosity is to be found in Southern England. After you have had your fill of such places as Germansweek, Clink, Turnerspuddle, Good Easter, Little Chart, Never Seen, and Sheepwash, you know you have reached the end of the line with the ultimate place name when you get to Land's End. After that, what's left?

Pronouncing some of England's town names is also likely to tongue-tie any toponymist. For instance, Woolfardisworthy is officially called Woolzry, whereas Alresford and Owslesbury are Alsford and Usslbry. Warwick is Worr'k, Leicester is Lester, Chiswick is Chis'k, Cirencester is Sisseter, Towcester is Toaster, Slaithwaite is Slowit, Sawbridgeworth is Sapsworth and Pontefract is Pomfrey. Had enough? Well, you go to the head of the class if you can figure this one out: In Kent the town named Romney is called Rummy but in Hampshire a town that is also named Romney is called Rumzy. But if that doesn't throw you, the town of Mapledurham will. Are you ready? It's pronounced Mum—that's the word!

11

A WORLD MARBLES CHAMPIONSHIP

WHO SAID marbles was a game for kids?

It is and has always been a game for men and, if Tinsley Green has anything to say about it, it will always remain a game for grown-up males. Here in this Sussex town, a few miles south of London's Gatwick Airport, the annual World Marbles Championships are held every Good Friday—a tourist-tantalizing tradition that is approximately four hundred years old.

Any male over the age of twenty-one can compete—so that lets the youngsters out, though they are allowed to stand on the sidelines and root for dad as he keeps the ball rolling in a game that has been played since the time of the ancient Greeks. The yearly Tinsley Green competition, however, goes back to the early sixteenth century when two men were vying for the hand of the same maiden who lived in this town. Having competed in archery, tree-felling, a variety of races and wrestling, which all ended in impressive ties, the two suitors agreed to prove their mettle in a game of marbles. The man who proved the better marble player finally won the bride. Since the crucial contest had been held on a Good Friday, Tinsley Green has been staging a marbles championship every year since then on that day.

Today, the prize is no longer the hand of a pretty damsel but a baby pig, a firkin of ale and a large medal proclaiming the victor the World's Champion Marble Player. The current champ is Len Smith, a steel worker in his fifties who, in the past, has copped the title as many as seven times in a row. Champion Smith's hottest challengers are several delightfully eccentric competitors who, from time to time, manage to wrest the honors away from him. There is, for instance, Wee Willie Wright, a pensioner famous for coming to the annual duel with a miniature hot water bag attached to his jacket to keep his "shooting thumb" warm. Then there is Bernard Wilcock, the Duke of Norfolk's tailor, admired because he always plays with a cigar in his mouth. Several years ago, when a prankish spectator stole the man's cheroot, he refused to knuckle down to the event. Then, after the organizers supplied him with a substitute Havana (not entirely to his liking, however), Mr. Wilcock made his initial shot a beauty and went on to win the match hands down.

The rules of Tinsley Green's migs marathon are quite simple. Thirteen agates are scattered in a sandy ring that is six feet in diameter and the first player to hit seven marbles out of the pot with his "shooting marble" is proclaimed the champ. The regulations also state that when a player shoots, four knuckles must touch the ground. For the team competition, the rules are a bit different. There are six players on each squad, and the first team that knocks twenty-five marbles out of a total of forty-nine scattered wins the crown. The marble teams usually have colorful names, such as the Handcross Bulldogs, the Copthorne Spitfires, the Ergs or the Terrible Toucans.

Whether he competes with a team or individually, a man's "shooting marble" is something special, because he usually has taken the trouble of making it himself. For instance, Len Smith's shooter, which is worth (to him) $240, was fashioned from the porcelain of his kitchen sink. He ground it down with emery boards until it was precisely .725ths of an inch in diameter and perfectly round. Most of the shooters are glass, however.

Several years ago, one rapscallion tried to put something over by entering the tournament with a steel ball that had been painted to look like a glass marble. Unmasked by the judges, the cur was barred from appearing at the Tinsley Green games for life.

One of the best shooters was owned by the late Sam Spooner, a showy nonagenarian who was a crowd favorite. His was ground from solid marble that came from Carrara, Italy, and he often gave post-tournament demonstrations with it. Shortly before his death, Mr. Spooner could fire his shooter with such impelling force and velocity that, from ten feet, he would shatter a drinking glass.

They don't make 'em like old Sam anymore and at the annual games now the fans miss him very much. The likeable contestant stood as a perfect example of the town's main theme—that to win all the marbles you have to have a Tinsley Green thumb.

Marbles champion Len Smith during the annual World Marbles competition (PHOTO COURTESY OF CRAWLEY & DISTRICT OBSERVER).

MEAN TIME

SOMETIMES it's just a matter of packaging. Ready or not, here comes Greenwich. It's the place where every visitor plays the same camera game. In utter delight, he stands with one foot in the Western Hemisphere and the other foot in the Eastern Hemisphere while the shutter records this mini-Herculean stunt.

On a map, run your finger to zero longitude (the prime meridian) and then to the latitude that reads 41 degrees, 28 minutes and 38 seconds north. That, folks, is the spot where East meets West. The place is Greenwich, a metropolitan borough of London, where, on top of a hill at the old Royal Observatory, you will find the line that divides the hemispheres. This is the position from which Greenwich mean time is derived.

The line splitting the two hemispheres is invisible, by the way. But in the forecourt of the observatory, in front of one of the buildings, there is an embedded brass strip that runs up to the wall, ending at a sealed glass door. Predictably, everybody who comes to see

Author Nino Lo Bello stands
with one foot in the Western Hemisphere
and the other foot in the
Eastern Hemisphere at Greenwich, England
(PHOTO BY IRENE ROONEY LO BELLO).

for himself has his photograph taken straddling the line with one foot in each hemisphere. Even travel writers have been known to do it.

Because clocks in the world are set in relation to Greenwich mean time, when you get here, don't let a minute go by. Can you think of a better place on earth to set your own watch? You can either regulate your timepiece from a twenty-four hour clock on the wall outside the observatory or from one that is inside. It runs according to an atomic clock that is accurate down to thousandths of millionths of a second.

Okay. But why Greenwich?

It all began some three hundred years ago or so when King Charles II started the Royal Observatory and appointed John Flamsteed as the Astronomer Royal. Out of an annual salary of approximately three hundred dollars, which wasn't always paid, and with money from his own pocket, Britain's first astronomer had to buy parts to make his own equipment. Although hampered by the meager funds at his disposal, Flamsteed made the best of his situation and managed to get his instruments set up to study the moon and stars.

Nobody in that era had invented a clock accurate enough to tell sailors how far east or west they were and Flamsteed sought ways to find a reliable method of calculating longitude. To pursue this goal, he hired a twenty-year-old youth by the name of Edmond Halley to go to the island of St. Helena to make precise star maps of the southern skies—the same Halley who later discovered the famous comet named after him.

After succeeding Flamsteed as England's Astronomer Royal, Halley continued the research and began timing the pathways of the moon across the meridian in the hope that these observations would someday be useful in determining longitude at sea. They were.

Because Britain had done most of the pioneer work in this field at Greenwich, a decision was made to set 0° at Greenwich and since 1884 all countries have reckoned longitude that way. Inasmuch as local mean solar time depends on longitude, every nation quickly adopted Greenwich mean time for air and sea navigation.

Under the control of the British Admiralty, the Greenwich observatory has since 1838 carried on regular meteorological and magnetic observations and has made pictures of the sun almost every day since 1873. In 1946, however, because of air pollution and the glare of London's sky at night from street lights and neon signs, officials chose to relocate the observatory staff at Hurstmonceux Castle in Sussex where the atmosphere is better for telescope observations.

Greenwich (pronounced Gren'-itch and meaning "green dwellings") is the home of the National Maritime Museum and the Royal Naval College. King Henry VIII, Queen Mary and Queen Elizabeth I were born in Greenwich, at the royal residence whose site is now a hospital. Two of England's most renowned ships, the *Cutty Sark* and the *Gipsy Moth IV*, are both dry-docked at the local pier and for a small fee you can visit and wander around the decks of these vessels.

But, as far as the whole world is concerned, Greenwich is the place where time does stand still—because everyone knows that the village on the south bank of the Thames is marking time in the mean time.

"MR. CORK"

IF IT IS TRUE that a cork is usually in a tight spot, then it is also true that "Mr. Cork" is in the right spot. Sooner or later, every traveler who comes to Portugal discovers the jovial, five-by-five proprietor of "The House of Cork" on Lisbon's busy Rua da Escola Politecnica No. 4, which draws more tourists than any monument or site in this Atlantic-washed capital.

Mr. Cork runs a unique shop here. The doors, walls, floor and ceiling of his store are made of cork, which is logical when you consider he sells an elaborate variety of items made out of Portugal's most famous export. Mr. Cork's merchandise includes such things as cork stationery, cork picture frames, cork playing cards, cork suitcases, cork shoes, cork chess sets, cork ladies' handbags, cork dishes, cork postcards, cork pottery, cork doilies and about eight-hundred other different cork knicknacks and items.

He even invents new uses for cork, making new bestsellers for his store. For instance, Mr. Cork manufactures a floating bar for swimming pools complete with cork ice-bucket for people who want a drink while they are taking a dip. Though it is one of the most expensive items in the shop, it sells well.

The man who is known as Mr. Cork throughout Portugal is septuagenarian A. Gama Reis who is miffed if you call him Mr. Reis (it is part of his act!). That goes for his wife Luisa Maria who, it should surprise no one, goes under the sobriquet of "Mrs. Cork." About forty thousand people a year visit their shop and to each of them Mr. Cork serves a friendly glass of port. That's his style. He is a warm, outgoing man who

radiates good will in several languages, especially English, which he speaks quite well. His spirited handshake is but a sample of his Portuguese cordiality and, whether you buy or do not buy, Mr. Cork will fill your pockets with cork gift-souvenirs of all types, including the special Mr. Cork glass the port was served in.

Mr. Cork has a special affection for Americans, bordering on the fierce. It is understandable. As a child during the First World War, he lived in the Azores and, after the U.S. Marines landed there, he got a job with them (which helped him perfect his Yank lingo, including all the Stateside slang), serving as handyman, guide and interpreter. When the dreaded flu epidemic struck the Azores and people were dying like flies, the Americans saved his life and the lives of his family by supplying him with medicines and food. And, in 1954, when he went completely blind and had to run "The House of Cork" groping in darkness, it was an American medical doctor who took a personal and professional interest in his case and restored his sight with surgery. For such things is Mr. Cork eternally grateful to Americans.

Though his business is selling cork, it sometimes seems his main business is giving aid and succor to American visitors, be they tourists who are low in funds or military personnel who are flat broke. Because he can always tell when an American is strapped for cash, Mr. Cork sympathetically forces loans on these people and, he says, "Every single penny I have ever lent out has been repaid!"

"My whole life is wrapped around

Lisbon's "Mr. Cork" in front of his shop.

cork," adds Mr. Cork, who is one of the world's great experts on the light material. "Did you know that cork comes from the bark of an evergreen oak and that, during its 150 years of life, a cork tree may be stripped of its bark only once every ten years and then only during the summer months?" Natural cork, he explains, contains millions of tiny air cells per square inch, so that more than half of its weight is made up of air. Portugal produces almost half the world's supply of cork and exports to the United States alone about ten million dollars' worth.

Mr. Cork got into the cork line after he left the Azores at eighteen to go to the University of Lisbon. To help pay his tuition, he found a job with a cork company and it proved to be the turning point of his life. Once having advanced to district manager, he then suggested the idea of a shop devoted entirely to the sale of items made of cork. Although his superiors laughed at him, in 1948 he went ahead and opened up the *Casa da Corticas* (House of Cork) on his own. He now has 130

people working for him in various parts of the country carving his offbeat cork specialties. About ten years ago the Museum of Modern Art in New York selected a set of dishes he had created himself and put them on exhibit.

Earning better than $50,000 a year, Mr. Cork can boast of such customers as the late President Eisenhower, Winston Churchill and Cardinal Spellman, not to mention every movie star or celebrity who has ever been to Lisbon. John Wayne, for instance, ordered several thousand dollars' worth of cork geegaws and had Mr. Cork print this inscription on them: STOLEN FROM JOHN WAYNE.

Both Dallas and New Orleans have made Mr. Cork an honorary citizen, whereas the United States Marine Corps went so far as to designate him an honorary sergeant. They turned the tables on him by giving him a set of chevrons and hashmarks made out of cork! It took the Portuguese storekeeper by surprise—but even he had to admit it was a corking good idea.

17

*"Spanish Village"
in Barcelona.*

SPAIN IN
ONE AFTERNOON

INSTANT SPAIN!

How would you like to spend a few hours visiting every nook and cranny of Spain in one fell swoop? It can be done at what may be the cleverest tourist creation anywhere in the world, the "Spanish Village" in the heart of Barcelona.

With the aim of reproducing the most characteristic aspects of Spain accurately and according to the old geographic divisions of the country, this Catalan port city erected the *"Pueblo Español"* ("Spanish Village") in 1929 at the time of the International Exhibition of Barcelona. It was such a success that the city council decided to make it a permanent exhibit. Today it draws more tourists, Spaniards and foreigners alike, than any of Barcelona's other attractions. It provides in a few acres a chance to visit thoroughly authentic reproductions (full size but in a compact way) of houses, fountains and squares from every region of Spain, together with workshops illustrating the traditional crafts of the people from these provinces.

Looking through open windows and doorways, you can watch coppersmiths, silversmiths, lace-workers, glassblowers, embroiderers, wrought iron manufacturers, toymakers, potters, engravers, wood-painters, leather artisans, miniature shop builders, basket weavers and other craftsmen from every part of Spain.

From the center of Barcelona it is a short cab ride to the *Pueblo Español* which is located at the foot of the storied Montjuich Hill. One enters through the "Door of St. Vincent" (the famous door of the walls of Ávila), which has been meticulously reproduced stone by stone. Before you know it, you find yourself in a typical small town of Valencia. Tarry as long as you want in Valencia, but in less time than it takes to tell, you walk a few yards and now you are standing in a square in Córdoba. A little while later you are in front of a house in Cantabrico, which you leave by way of a typical street in Teruel. This leads you to the celebrated stairway of Santiago. Continue a bit more and you are forthwith inside the cloister of Burgos. Leave Burgos and immediately a lighthouse from Altana confronts you. In short order you will be visiting a Castilian patio, a Catalan house facade, a belltower from Ebro, a narrow Andalusian street, and so forth.

One idea that should be dispelled about the *Pueblo Español* is that its structures are made of cardboard or plaster or that any of the buildings are miniature in size. No, indeed! Every building was created out of real bricks, old wood, worked iron, authentic ceramic, dried Spanish mud and what-have-you. Moreover, everything is life-size yet, somehow, by some miracle of planning, everything fits together in a homogeneous way.

Covering these thousands and thousands of miles on foot, just by eating up a few yards here and a few yards there, a visitor can acquire marvelous souvenirs direct from the artisan. For instance, you can watch a Catalan glassblower make one of his magnificent creations in front of your eyes or a Toledo goldsmith fashion a sword or a pair of his famed scissors.

Among the most sensational buys of all, however, are the original manuscript pages from old Bibles and volumes that were printed and illustrated by monks' hands during the fifteenth century. Why the Spanish government allows these irreplaceable treasures to be sold, instead of placing them in museums where they belong, escapes all logic. But an alert tourist, faced with such a once in a lifetime opportunity, should get in on this while they last.

Whatever else the Spanish Village means to a tourist, it is enough to give your camera a positive outlook on Spanish life.

DON QUIJOTE SLEPT HERE

"DON QUIJOTE slept here!"

Even though he appeared in print over three and a half centuries ago, Don Quijote is alive and well and living in La Mancha. He is, in fact, alive, well and living in just about every town, village and hamlet of Spain. Don Quijote rides tall in this country just about every day of the week.

But here in Spain's La Mancha region, it seems Don Quijote rides a little taller than anywhere else. For Cervantes' odd nobleman (quixotic, if you prefer) has slipped out of the pages of the world's most published novel and has become a historical personage, better known and more endearing than any of Spain's array of royal monarchs. That also goes for his roly-poly sidekick, Sancho Panza, his horse, Rocinante, and his ineluctable girl friend, Dulcinea. Go anywhere in this region and to any town remotely connected with the wanderings of the Cervantes hero and you are likely to come across places called Tavern of Don Quijote, the Inn of Sancho Panza or the Wineshop of Dulcinea. In one location a blacksmith has proudly named his business establishment, the Place of Rocinante.

Here in El Toboso, which is in the heart of the La Mancha region and which was the home of Dulcinea (a half-day horseback ride from Don Quijote's hometown, Argamasilla de Alba), you come to get your best feel of the Don Quijote-La Mancha syndrome. El Toboso is a sleepy village that has been bypassed by the railroads and the highways, ignored by time and by the river, and left bereft of everything but literary notoriety. Yet it has attained tourist status among the Spaniards who chuckle at the mere mention of the name, which is a kind of standard Spanish joke. Mostly, tourists come to visit Dulcinea's house (despite her fictional birth) and to see the windmill.

You won't find many windmills left in Spain but, no matter where you go, you will find Don Quijote. You will find bookend Don Quijotes, ceramic tile Don Quijotes, carpet Don Quijotes and miles upon miles of store-shelf statue Don Quijotes, made of clay, tin, wood, bronze, cardboard, iron, sugar, aluminum, chocolate, silver, soap, gold and what have you. One town in this region, Santiago de Compostela, bases its entire economy on Don Quijote. Nearly all of the inhabitants, who are artisans, dedicate themselves to carving wooden figurines of the scrawny old undoer of wrongs and protector of virtue and honor. Some of these statuettes sell for as much as one-hundred dollars, though many are priced for as little as two dollars.

When *Don Quijote de La Mancha* was first published in 1605, it ran into six editions the first year. Today, next to the Bible, it is the world's most published and best-known book, having been translated into every known language. Because it has been in the public domain for many years, *Don Quijote* comes out every year in Spanish in at least ten different editions and it is said that there is not a single home in all Spain which does not have at least one copy of the book.

Inasmuch as it has no well-defined

Don Quijote and Sancho Panza in El Toboso.

boundaries and is neither a province nor a territorial unit, Spain's La Mancha region is not the kind of place to attract that type of tourist addicted to the beach umbrella. The map indicates it as a vast plain that extends from the mountains of Toledo and is a rather vague stretch of parched flat wilderness south of Madrid and east of Ciudad Real. There are no cities in the La Mancha sector. At best, you will find a few villages and a scattering of a half dozen market towns. The landscape is monotonous as you drive through the sunbaked ocean of terrain that looks like high noon on the Sahara Desert. Even more disappointing is the absence of windmills, "whom" Don Quijote engaged in "fierce and unequal battle." Of the hundreds of windmills that used to exist, the handful that still remain are to be found near the town of Campo de Criptana. Today they serve purely decorative purposes, since they stopped turning about seventy years ago.

Where the good knight saw giants once upon a time, La Mancha provides a twist. Bereft of functioning windmills, Spain has made a giant out of Don Quijote.

*Corner of Güell Park
created by Antonio Gaudi.*

THE
ECCENTRIC
ARCHITECT
OF BARCELONA

ONLY THIS CITY, the largest port on the Mediterranean, which takes a kind of tribal pride in being unlike the rest of Spain and which proudly thumbs its civic nose at Madrid, could have given birth and leeway to the most unusual architect of them all. Any tourist who comes here can't avoid him and after awhile every tourist cannot get enough of him.

There may yet be a few people in Barcelona who do think Antonio Gaudi was mad. But whatever one thinks of Gaudi's state of mental stability, or lack of it, nearly everybody in Barcelona feels the same about him; he is loved and adored and admired and analyzed and bragged about. It is said in Barcelona that you have not really seen Barcelona until you have visited this architect's unique creations.

Gaudi "elaborated in three dimensions impulses which today most architects would dissipate on the analyst's couch." Having thrived around the turn of the century, he may have indeed been an architectural genius; yet his scattered structures around this city show that he was really less an architect and more a brilliant exterior decorator. No matter how many pictures you see of Gaudi's stuff, nothing can quite prepare you for your first confrontation with a Gaudi building. It will remind you of a sand castle over which a wave has just washed or a structure made of ice cream which has begun to melt in the sun.

The Gaudi works are spread all over the Barcelona map. To seek them out, you would have to hire a taxicab or buy yourself a bicycle to do it all. And do it all you must, for a little Gaudi is like eating one salted peanut—you always want more. So let's start with the Güell park in the north end of the city on the slopes of the Tibidabo Hill. Commissioned by the wealthy industrialist Eusebio Güell in 1900 as a gift to the city, the park took fourteen years to complete. This is a unique children's playground with hanging gardens, fairy caverns, arcades of insanely tilting pillars, terraces of multicolored tiles and rows of giant cannonballs—everything suggestive of things to eat like lollipops and sherbet. Some of the crooked columns will remind you of chocolate twists with marshmallow filling. With its ceramic lizards hung on concrete stalactites, its improbable landscapes of mazes, queer duck fountains, bright ceramic benches, Hansel and Gretel houses and serpentine mosaic benches, the Güell park would make the ultimate in a setting for a Fellini film—particularly the outdoor urinal topped by a dunce cap.

Gaudi's apartment house, nicknamed "The Quarry," on the Paseo de Gracia has balconies that droop and windows that resemble the entrance to caves. The chimneys are hooded in hats of concrete so that they look like cottages for Walt Disney dwarfs. Inside, the corridors are not carpeted but cobbled and the rooms have been laid out in every shape—trapezoidal, triangular, pentagonal—anything but square or rectangular.

Although Gaudi's flamboyant architectural constructions seem to be reckless in concept while showing the intensely personal touch of the man, his most overwhelming monument remains his unfinished church of the Sagrada Familia. Representing ideas that have literally gone beserk, the incomplete cathedral has only one facade completed so far—a facade crowned by spires looking like zeppelins with air vents. Lizards peer at you from everywhere, turkeys gobble from the porticos, giant columns rest on the backs of turtles, a battalion of outsized snails lies in waiting. By all means take the dizzying elevator that goes up the center of the colossus and walk along the catwalks where you can ogle close up other platforms covered with fruit, vegetables, seaweed, a T-square, a boat, an anchor, a saw and who-knows-what. Some tourists have called these bewildering Gaudi gimcracks everything from a "vegetable jungle" to a "Wagnerian overture in stone." Gaudi's equally eccentric compatriot, Salvador Dali, once called the odd basilica "a cathedral cooked by a schizoid angel." Look who's talking. . . .

Before he died in 1926, when he absentmindedly walked into the path of a clanging trolley, Gaudi gave the world dozens of spooky chimneys, innumerable cockeyed sets of furniture and his "House of Bones." Don't miss it if you can!

WHISTLE WHILE YOU WORK

THERE IS AN OLD SAW (not true) that you find no canaries in the Canary Islands. But the inhabitants of Gomera—a chunk of volcanic archipelago which is the least visited of the Canary Islands—whistle like canaries because that is the way people talk here.

The name of this whistle lingo is "Silbo," and it is used by the people who live in the interior regions of Gomera when they want to speak to each other over long distances. Because there are deep ravines that chop up the island and the terrain in general is so rugged, the language of whistling was developed so that neighbors could talk with each other without making an arduous trek that could eat up a whole day—even when the distance involved might be less than a mile.

Developed several centuries ago, Silbo can be used for stretches of up to eight miles when atmospheric conditions do not interfere. Gomera, being an island, can get windy sometimes from the Atlantic, but wind or no wind, whistle-talk can go on with no difficulties even if the speakers are two to three miles away from each other. Here in Gomera it·is said (without documentation, however) that Christopher Columbus also learned how to talk in whistles. It seems he spent a great deal of time here because he loved the solitude and allegedly "he loved the wife of Gomera's governor."

Whether Silbo can be classified technically as a language is something on which linguistic anthropologists do not agree. The fact stands that it is infinitely more than just a series of sibilant signals to communicate a simple message or a glossary of common phrases limited in scope. A tourist who takes the trouble to come here—and it is indeed worth any bother—can see (or hear) for himself the rather complicated conversations that can be carried on through Silbo. It's fun just to stand around and eavesdrop on people miles apart as they exchange local gossip, report on the latest news, give instructions to workers, send their orders to a store in the next village and whisssssssssssssssstle just about everything that other folks say with spoken words.

This writer, exercising professional skepticism about the whole thing, put Silbo to a hard test. He typed up a complicated paragraph in Spanish and had a Gomeran whistle out the paragraph into a tape recorder. Later, in another part of the island, he chose a Gomeran at random, played for him the taped Silbo message and was given, word for word, the contents of the original paragraph.

Every Gomeran grows up learning Spanish, of course, but many also learn Silbo along the way as a second language. The kids do just fine with Silbo by the age of seven and, in some cases, even make friends with peers miles away whom they have never met. The Gomerans will tell you that young men oftentimes have dated young girls through Silbo, girls they have not yet seen in person. These youths maintain they can tell if Dolores is pretty merely by the way way she toots her phrases. On this island, a gal does not mind if a man whistles at her.

Because it could take a person several hours to travel a mere hundred yards

To communicate, some residents of Gomera have to use whistle-talk
(PHOTO COURTESY SPANISH GOVERNMENT TOURIST OFFICE).

over the rocky chasms and steep rises of Gomera, the natives also have a unique way of covering such tricky distances quickly. They sometimes use long sticks and pole vault their way from one place to another. The poles save wear and tear on the feet and, when used by the skillful Gomerans, actually speed up transportation many times over.

Boasting a temperature that never goes below 60° the year round, Gomera has a rain forest (one of two in the world) with grotesque tree shapes that are among the weirdest anywhere. To visit some of the best spots of this primeval relic, ask for taxidriver Juan Barrosa in the port town of San Sebastián; he knows how to negotiate the narrow mountain roads, especially the parts that have no shoulders. Señor Barrosa will also take you to visit Gomerans who live in the interior, the cave dwellers. Renowned for their hospitality, these are the hardy natives who speak Silbo—people who really whistle while they work.

25

Mudsloggers.

THE MUDSLOGGERS OF HOLLAND

IF JOGGING is becoming the favorite health sport of the western world, here's another health sport, virtually unknown outside the Netherlands, that will tax your thighs better than jogging or its puff-puff variations. In Dutch, it's called "Wadlopen" (which means mudslogging) and, if you try your hand at it (your feet, to be more exact), then here's mud in your eye.

So come to Wierum, a tiny town two-hundred miles northeast of Amsterdam on the Friesland coast of Holland where, with some three dozen fellow wadlopers, led by veteran wadloping guides, you can slog your way through North Sea mud for two and a half hours to a mud desert island five miles away for a picnic lunch and then ooze your way back through the same earthy glop for another two and a half hours. Hmmm, who needs jogging already, when wadlopen may be the next "in" thing in health sports?

Geert Jan de Weert, a fifty-year-old hydro-engineer, is the organizer and main guide of the Saturday morning wadlopen trips for which advance reservations should be made, because no more than sixty people at a time can go on a wadlop expedition. He can be reached by telephone at 05199–224 or by mail at Kerkplein 2, Wierum, Holland. Once you are booked, he will send you an instruction folder in English explaining what you will need and where and when you are to meet and how to get there.

First and foremost is your footwear. Sneakers are absolutely required, as no other type of footgear is acceptable, not even bare feet. Heavier footgear becomes mud-logged and will drag you down perilously, whereas a pair of sneakers won't do that and also protect your feet from sharp clam shells.

Walking shorts or bathing suits are strongly advised, as are warm shirts or sweaters under a weather-proof jacket, because it is usually much colder out on the mudflats than on shore. Also bring along some extra dry clothing packed snugly in a sealed plastic bag.

To insure maximum safety, wadlopen trips are never made unless weather conditions are just right. These are determined by a complicated set of scientific instruments on the Friday afternoon before a Saturday morning departure. The season for wadlopen runs from May into September during which period there are usually two trips made on Saturdays.

One is to the island of Engelsmanplaat which would-be wadlopers, who have not yet had their baptism of mud, are advised to try first. Engelsmanplaat is an uninhabited island that rises about four inches above sea level when the tide is out and disappears quite soon as the tide begins to come in. Lunch (a "Dutch treat") is taken here while you sit on a mud bank contemplating an occasional jellyfish or sandworms doing their thing. With a lunch-break that can only last a half hour, your guide will get all of you back onto the mud for the return trek to the mainland, because the tidewaters soon begin to erase Engelsmanplaat until it reappears the next day at about the same time.

The other Saturday trip is to a bigger island called Ameland. This is a much tougher destination to get to, though the distance is shorter, and it too takes about two and a half hours. However, instead of mud-walking your way back to Wierum, you pick up a public ferry. Some people prefer to swim home from Ameland, but this is discouraged by de Weert.

Is wadlopen really dangerous?

Well, yes—if you try to do it on your own. The guide who takes you, in addition to carrying emergency equipment strapped to his back, keeps in constant contact with shore on his walkie-talkie. He also knows where the quicksand risks lie and where the invisible "holes" are that could swallow you completely before anybody is even aware you are no longer with the group. The main danger, of course, is that tricky North Sea tide on which de Weert is generally considered to be the world's greatest expert. So what the man says, you do!

There is another wadlopen "danger"—if you want to call it that. This is a situation in which you bog down into the mud, sometimes even up to your neck, though more likely up to your hips. This sinking feeling is avoidable if you keep moving at a fairly energetic pace. Once you get caught that way in a mud-prison, your guide knows what to do to extricate you and get you going again. You learn quickly that your feet, calves, knees, thighs and every muscle of locomotion must not ever tarry once, as you tramp, waddle, slosh, creep, crawl, wobble and i-n-c-h your way.

Wadlopen is not a sport to get in Dutch with.

A BETTER NAME for this hamlet of Baarle is "Splitsville" because it is a wholly schizophrenic piece of geography. Half of the town lies in Holland, half in Belgium. In all Europe—and perhaps in the whole wide world—there is no more looney situation than is to be found here.

Because Baarle is part Dutch and part Belgian, it has two mayors, two town halls, two police forces, two telephone systems, two post offices, two flags, two different income tax rates, two separate military service regulations and even two names for the same town—Baarle-Nassau (which is in Holland) and Baarle-Hertog (which is in Belgium). There's more. Silly as it may sound, you even have such harrowing situations where one part of a house is in one country and the other part of the same house is in another country. For instance, there is the home of Adrianus Mathjssen where he and his wife sleep in Belgium, while his children in the next room sleep in Holland. As expected, Mr. Mathjssen has to pay real estate taxes to two countries. Under two different governments, this particular house must be served by two postal systems. Therefore it has two addresses. Another thing: the Holland-Belgium border happens to run right through the middle of the Mathjssen bathroom so that the sink is in Holland, the bathtub in Belgium. As yet, neither country has sought to erect a customs barrier at the john.

But the *reductio ad absurdum* is to be found in a cafe on Splitsville's main street. The new pool table in the bar straddles the frontier. Consequently, the billiard balls cross the border back and forth between Belgium and Holland a couple of thousand times a day. Each game is an "international match," but a player does not need a visa to knock an eightball into a side pocket.

One thing you do need in Baarle (Baarle-Nassau or Baarle-Hertog) is a sense of humor. Things can get ludicrous around here, yet sometimes the humor can be a bit ticklish. Consider the case of Mijnheer Theo Bloem, a medical doctor. He is qualified to practice surgery in Holland but not in Belgium. Because his dispensary is attached to his house which stands on the border, a few years ago the Belgian gov-

Roadway stripe in "Splitsville" is th

PIECE OF GEOGRAPHY

ernment decided he could not use the dispensary (all of which was in Belgium) to do surgery. Ordered to remove it, Dr. Bloem had to build a new one thirty feet away on Dutch soil. It cost him nearly $5,000.

The villagers of this hermaphroditic homogeneous hamlet have been living this way for over eight hundred years. Baarle's history is quite complicated, having to do with the twelfth century Lord of Breda ceding part of his landed estate to the Duke of Brabant after a dispute. The territorial parcel was broken up into small pieces between the two titled bullies and, by the 1648 Treaty of Westphalia, the land in Baarle that belonged to the Lord of

border between Holland and Belgium.

Breda was given to the northern province of the Greater Netherlands and the land owned by the Duke of Brabant to the southern province. Eventually these provinces became Holland and Belgium, but the nationality of 5,732 plots of ground was established separately. Over the years, however, a number of these plots came under single ownership so that some parcels of land, though half in Belgium and half in Holland, had homes erected on them.

"We do not really look upon ourselves as either Dutchmen or Belgians," declares Ingrid Koks, who works in the tourist office at the Hotel De Engel and who admits, if pressed, she is a citizen of Holland. "We all think of ourselves as Baarlenaars bût, of course, whichever nationality we have, we are subject to our country's laws." Miss Koks hastens to add, however, that because she and her fellow townsmen live in two different economies, she has the choice of buying cigarettes, for instance, at Belgian or Dutch prices (currently, Belgian cigarettes are a few cents cheaper because the state tax on them is lower than Holland's).

In the past, each time the two countries have initiated negotiations to resolve the political situation, the Baarlenaars have raised the loudest squawks and have threatened all kinds of fuss. Meanwhile, that Splitsville draws several hundred thousand curious, unbelieving, show-me tourists every year is a strong factor in keeping the statutes quo. Indeed, the natives of this loco locus are laughing all the way to the bank because their town borders on the ridiculous.

29

THE STILT-WALKERS OF NAMUR

SO IF IT'S TUESDAY and you're in Belgium and you're one of those tourists who drag their tales behind them, with or without the positive proof of a camera, this tiny town on the confluence of the Sambre and Meuse Rivers about thirty-six miles southwest of Brussels provides one of the craziest historical shows in all Europe, guaranteed to raise eyebrows and some questions as to how come.

We're talking about Namur's stilt-walkers. On a hill near the city limits, the stilt-walkers fight a folkloristic fight that will leave you laughing. It all seems a bit unbalanced as you watch the ten-foot giants confront one another in a serious and determined effort to knock each other to the ground, the whole shebang moving to the rhythmic beat of kettledrums and the blare of trumpets. Bedecked in original fourteenth-century costumes with floppy black medieval hats from which dangle blond curls, each participant gets cheers and jeers as he steers and veers.

The winner is the fellow who doesn't bite the dust, who survives all the elbow jabs and fist punches. When all the other combatants have fallen, the man who is still on his wooden pins in an upright position gets all the glory and fuss and the team he represents is the grand winner. Make no mistake about it, the whole thing is serious but pretty funny, too, depending on your standpoint.

Thanks to Namur's crazy-quilt history, based on the fact that it was in the past an impregnable citadel perched on an impossible-to-approach rock, stilt-walking is a fulltime hobby for many of the city's 32,000 citizens, who learn the art as children. Both men and women here know what they are doing when they perch themselves on their striped poles and walk, jog, run and skip hither and thither. Many a fine romance starts between him 'n' her when they meet for the first time on stilts on a Sunday afternoon promenade through the park, where it's been said that conversations are never . . . er, stilted.

And how indeed did the stilt become a lifestyle for Namur?

It seems, according to local history tracts, that a nobleman by the name of Jehan of Flanders, who was lord of the County of Namur back in the 1300s, laid siege to the town and sought to have the inhabitants capitulate by starving them. When town leaders begged him to desist, Count Jehan is quoted as having said: "No. There is no pardon, not even if you come on foot, on horseback, by wagon or boat!"

Because he left no other approach, the Namurians popped up with an idea. Down to the last adult, one day they approached Jehan on stilts—and the gimmick worked, for the Count was amused no end and he pardoned the people. But it did not end there. To commemorate the saving of Namur, an annual event was established in 1411 in which the stilt was given special honor as the central prop. To give the whole thing a bit of zest, the Namurians set up two teams of men who would fight each other on stilts.

One group, called the *"melans,"* was dressed in red and white and the other group, known as the *"avresses,"* was garbed in black and yellow. For centuries the festival went on. Unbelievably, however, during the eighteenth century, King Joseph II had a personal aversion for stilts and he decreed in 1789 that any man or woman who was found by the police using or possessing stilts would be publicly flogged and thrown into prison for six weeks. That didn't quite stop stilt-walking in Namur, though it did put the annual festival into "tilt."

Only in 1951 did Namur revive the stilt show because the wooden pole was such an integral part of its history. Today the folklore event is truly festive. The show starts with the twenty men facing each other in two lines of ten. Stilt-war rules allow contestants to use swift elbows or closed fists to knock down adversaries; they are also permitted to raise one stilt, deftly nudge and/or boot an enemy high-stepper to the ground. Anything goes, as a matter of fact, except the use of fingers (grabbing is illegal), which will disqualify a woody gladiator.

So if it's September and you're not in Belgium, it's high time to come here and see for yourself that the Belgians of Namur do stand on ceremony.

Stilts have played an important role in the history of the Belgian town whose citizens engage in the hobby of stilt-walking (PHOTO COURTESY OF SYNDICAT D'INITIATIVE ET DE TOURISME OF NAMUR).

WHERE NAPOLEON TUMBLED

A CHORE INDEED it would be to pinpoint a patch of land anywhere in Europe that played more of a decisive role in the history of the nineteenth century and had a greater influence on the course of a century's events than this name-fame battlefield where Napoleon tumbled.

Because this tiny town, which has not changed much since that fateful day (June 18, 1815), is only twelve miles from downtown Brussels, a go-go tourist would do himself a real injustice if he did not come here "to meet his Waterloo," compliments of Napoleon Bonaparte. And don't fret if you are rusty on history, because Waterloo will take care of any information gap and make an instant expert out of you.

The site of the time-honored battle, a rolling green pasture where 45,000 soldiers and 15,000 horses died in one day, can be viewed in toto from a huge cone of earth, atop which is a large bronze lion that has been cast from the

Waterloo.

cannons of the defeated French. There are only 226 steps (only?) to the top of the monument, but it won't be the huffing and the puffing that will leave you breathless. Up there, it does not take much to form a mental picture of the massed body of troops marching shoulder to shoulder in the face of point-blank cannon fire or of dapper cavalrymen with plumed silver helmets charging to fanfares of French trumpets and squeals of Scottish bagpipes. You have seen all this in the movies several times and you have also seen it in dozens of famous romantic paintings depicting the scene in which Napoleon's dream of a French-dominated Europe fizzled under the Duke of Wellington's strategy.

Around your high lookout there are plaques showing the positions of the French army and those of Wellington's combined forces. Helping you better to understand what happened during this great monumental battle that lasted from about 11:00 o'clock in the morning till 9:30 at night are a number of talk-guide machines and telescopes. The details can be condensed in a few sentences. There were more than 140,000 men and 30,000 horses involved but, after about ten hours of contact, the French had taken a clobbering—so that Napoleon's bid to get back what he had lost in his calamitous Russian campaign went up, literally, in smoke. The defeat meant exile for the little emperor on the island of St. Helena, but it brought Europe a half century of peace.

At Waterloo, Napoleon had planned to drive between the two major armies of Wellington, crush them separately and press on towards Brussels and Ghent. Each of Napoleon's five attacks that day was repulsed and, as night fell,

with the arrival of General Gebhard von Blücher and his Prussians, who waded into Napoleon's right flank, Wellington finished off the French with a massed thrust.

Whatever you may miss from the top of "The Lion of Waterloo" in the way of historical background, you will recoup down below, for there are several movie houses that show only one film over and over again—the story of the Battle of Waterloo. Connected to these Toonerville trolley theatres are museums, restaurants and souvenir shops where you can absorb your history in easy-to-take doses. Not far from the battlefield, one can also visit the farmhouse Bonaparte used as his headquarters and also the Wellington Museum, which is flanked by an iron gate wrought so that the date, 1815, stands out rather clearly if you go across the street for perspective. There is also a wax museum for those visitors who want to see what everybody important that day looked like.

Definitely one sight that should not be missed at Waterloo is Norbert Brassinne, a full-time collector of Napoleona. The restaurant he owns was built from the relics of the battlefield; he also has in a cardboard box a large collection of bones which his ancestors gathered after the battle. The Belgian government wants to buy these bones to put into a national museum, but Brassinne refuses all offers.

You won't have any difficulty finding the sixty-five-year-old eccentric, who happens also to have more than a thousand different books on the Emperor in his library. What distinguishes Brassinne from other people is his mode of dress, for he wears the uniform of a certain historical figure associated with Waterloo. Is it necessary to ask whose?

IT ALL BEGAN in the seventh century. Hopping. Not jogging, or running, or skipping. But hopping. And it happens every year on the first Tuesday in June following Pentecost that some ten thousand people come to Echternach in Luxembourg to hop for more than two miles through narrow streets and winding alleys in honor of St. Willibrord. Er . . . did you say hopping?

This elastic form of physical exertion, now a formalized ritual here, has a bit of history behind it that is a bit zany. But no more zany than the way the annual Hop Parade takes place in front of at least thirty thousand tourists who come from nearby Switzerland, Germany, France and the Low Countries to watch. As is inevitable, some of the watchers become infused with the morning-long proceedings and they themselves join in.

While holding on to a twisted piece of white cloth, the other end of which is held by a partner, the participants hop four abreast, three steps forward and two steps backward, one row moving to the left, the other row to the right. This odd procession begins right after the early Mass in the huge basilica, presided over by the leaders of the Catholic hierarchy.

And for what reason does all this collective hopping happen in honor of St. Willibrord? And which *Who* is he in the *Who's Who of Saints?*

Well, St. Willibrord is one of Luxembourg's big guns. For one thing, he is the miracle worker generally credited with having brought Christianity to the Teutons, a job that was, according to local historians, extremely tricky. But the Echternach hopping done in the name of St. Willibrord, who came down from the north of England to convert the pagans, is for yet another accomplishment.

Back in the seventh century, this hilly hamlet on the southwestern border of Germany was in the clutch of a plague, which now goes under the name of St. Vitus's dance in modern medicine. Willibrord had his own formula for fighting the plague and promised that, if the people subjected themselves to physical punishment and prayed, the illness would go away. To the tune of a jig-like melody he had brought from Northumberland, Willibrord got the locals to hop up and down until they collapsed from sheer exhaustion. Miraculously, the plague ended.

And Willibrord got credit for it.

So to this day the "Hopping Procession" (its official name) is carried out once a year, with a few modifications. The same English tune that Willibrord introduced is still played for the hoppers' benefit over and over again. Now there are several musical combos— some with fiddles, some with horns, some with accordions—which march along, repeating the haunting ancient refrain. Although it is not the official "anthem" of Echternach, the song, after thirteen centuries, still remains perennially number one on the Luxembourg hit parade.

Lying on the banks of the River Sure, which forms the frontier with Germany, the slumberous town of Echternach is surrounded by woods that are crisscrossed with hundreds of footpaths,

Luxembourg's annual Hop Parade takes place before some 30,000 tourists who come to watch, some of whom join in (PHOTO COURTESY OF OFFICE NATIONAL DU TOURISME LUXEMBOURG).

the delight of hikers seeking arboreal solitude and quiet. Although behind the next clump of oaks you might not actually meet Hansel and Gretel, a visit into the forest will lead you to waterfalls, rock promontories and dozens of magnificent views of the Sure, which provides river bathing, fishing and canoeing.

With a population of 3,500, Echternach retains a remarkably medieval atmosphere, its old patrician houses, narrow streets and ancient ramparts providing the props for perhaps one of the most impressive settings anywhere. The basilica of Echternach, which is the most important religious building in the country, houses a magnificent white marble sarcophagus containing the remains of St. Willibrord. The vaults are painted with frescoes that go back to 1100 A.D.

Though the annual hoopla over the hopla comes to an end at midday, the festival itself continues into the evening with a noontime gastronomic interlude. You would have to reserve in advance for a table in Echternach's best restaurant at the Hotel du Commerce. Celebrated for its outstanding kitchen and two regional specialities (smoked rack of pork and fresh trout from the Sure baked with almonds in a white wine sauce), the hotel also thrusts forth other delectable items.

Try the house-cured ham, their homemade sausages and their splendiferous local lagers that even Germany itself envies. About the beer, you can easily understand why it's better than best. After all, Echternach knows its malts—and even more about its hops.

THE MYSTERY OF THE STONE COFFIN

IF YOU ARE the kind of tourist who likes a pinch of mystery during your travels, then there is a special sort of treat in store for you in a wooded mountain town within winking distance of the Spanish frontier. For here in the Eastern Pyrenees you can exercise some deductive powers at solving what is perhaps the most "mysterious mystery" in all touristdom.

Arles-sur-Tech is noted as a folklore center. During Holy Week, for example, curious sightseers come to watch the traditional parade of hooded penitents as they whip themselves mercilessly to the mournful roll of muffled drums. But, on the River Tech, which runs through the Valley of Vallespir towards the Mediterranean, the biggest attraction is "The Mystery."

Of the thousands and thousands of tourists who pop in every year, including the bountiful number of self-styled Sherlock Holmes skeptics, none has yet solved the mystery of the marble tomb that stands outside the abbey-church of Sainte-Marie, which was founded by Charlemagne in the eighth century. Several decades ago, a notary public of Arles deposited a thousand gold francs with the city treasury to be awarded to any person able to explain away the mystery of the discolored sarcophagus. So far, no takers.

Dating from the fourth century, the sarcophagus to the left of the central doorway of the Sainte-Marie church seems no different from any other stone box of the same period. But for over a thousand years it has kept under wraps a riddle baffling all comers. For reasons that defy all manner of explanation, the ancient shell produces a pure, clear water which is drinkable.

Although the marble container has a maximum capacity of forty-four gallons, nearly 160 gallons of the translucent fluid drip forth each year. This is collected into tiny, bulbous bottles, and natives swear that there are remarkable medicinal benefits for those who sip some of it.

In the year 1794, according to the city records of Arles, an official committee of clergymen, lawyers and town officials examined the heavy box at great length in the presence of the town's eitizenry. The coffin was suspended. No lead pipes or holes were detected by anybody. The stone that supported it was not porous. Yet,

Marble tomb at Arles-sur-Tech is the center of a mystery over a thousand years old (PHOTO BY TANYA GIVENS RILEY).

though the test continued over a period of several days, the tomb kept on secreting water. Moreover, it was established by scientific analysis that the sarcophagus fluid was of a chemical composition not to be found in any of the waters of this region. The liquid itself appears to be distilled.

Some doubting Thomases have asserted that the whole thing is a hoax, that monks or fanatic laymen secretly replenish the water supply when nobody is around. But it is not easy to be able to fool people consistently for over ten centuries this way, particularly since skeptics time and again have set themselves as hidden spies and watched the coffin day and night.

Originally, according to legend, the stone vessel was brought to Arles from Rome on the back of a mule. Containing relics from the grave of the Persian martyrs, Abdon and Sennen, it was a gift of Pope John XII in the year 960. So as not to attract thieves, the sarcophagus was hidden in a wooden barrel filled with water. When the mule reached its destination, the local cleric put some barrel water into the marble casket. Since that time the flow of liquid from the sarcophagus has not ceased. Every year for centuries Arles-sur-Tech celebrates a feast-rite on July 30th, during which water from the sanctified container is distributed in tiny plastic bottles to people who believe it will make improvements in their health, especially with intestinal, cardiac and rheumatic ailments.

Although most foreign tourists who visit here give little or no credence to the water's alleged curative properties, not one person has been able to offer a logical explanation for the perpetual flow. Those who do come up with some kind of theory, however watered down it may be, are invariably all wet.

37

A VILLAGE THE NAZIS BURNED ALIVE

NOT A SOUL LIVES in Oradour-sur-Glane and this is the stark drama that screams out at you. You walk along the empty streets of this historic village which the Nazis burned alive during the Second World War and you are reminded, step by step, as you roam among the charred ruins, of the incredible human tragedy that makes this place perhaps the most macabre tourist site in the world.

Six hundred and forty-two persons of whom 247 were children (virtually everyone who lived here, except six survivors), were shot or burned to death on June 10, 1944, by the famous "Das Reich" S.S. division in revenge for the guerrilla murder of a German officer. So that the world will never forget, the French keep the burned-out town as a national monument.

A new, modern Oradour has sprung up a few hundred yards away from the wall-enclosed ruin that spreads over 300 acres. At the entrance of the wrecked village are two signs that speak volumes: one reads "SCENE OF EXECUTION" and the other says "SILENCE." Behind these signs is a church with broken windows and destroyed belfry and beyond lies the silent skeleton of a town. The stage is set for your visit to one of the grisliest sights in all Europe. Booklets and folders giving historical details of the massacre, as well as color slides and other mementos, are available in a souvenir shop that has been set up in a shack near the entrance. If nothing else, a stop here before you proceed will help you understand better the stark message of Oradour—that war engenders inhuman and unhuman crime against human beings, crimes committed because war is the business of barbarians.

No historian is quite sure why Oradour-sur-Glane, fifteen miles north of Limoges, was selected by the commanding officer of the S.S. unit, General Bernard Heinz Lammerding. Certain it is that Oradour did not house any of France's underground Maquis fighters, for it was off the beaten path and most of the residents had never even seen a German soldier. But Oradour was picked for the reprisal.

It was a Saturday afternoon, just after lunchtime, and the sun was shining when trucks full of storm troopers rumbled into Oradour. Everybody in town was quickly rounded up and paraded into the public square. The men were kept to one side; the women and children were led away. The mayor was asked to single out fifty residents to be shot. He refused, answering defiantly: "I name myself—and if that is not sufficient, then also my family." This was not enough for the major in charge of the detail. He had all the men ushered into barns and sheds where they were machine-gunned. Though some of the victims were not killed outright, the Nazis spread straw over them and set fire to it so that those who were not dead were cremated.

Meanwhile, the women and children who had been packed into the village church met a similar fate. All of them were cut down by machine gun bursts and then the church was put to flame. To make sure there were no survivors, every building was set ablaze. Only five men and one woman survived the massacre—but of these only the woman actually witnessed any of

*Burned-out Oradour
stands today as the Nazis left it.*

the horror. Her name is Marguerite
Rouffange and she lives in virtual isolation just off the main square of New
Oradour, refusing to this day to see
anyone or allow any photographers to
take any pictures of her.

Madame Rouffange, a farmer's wife,
watched her small son, two daughters
and a seven-month-old grandchild die
under a hail of lead inside the church.
She also lost her husband. Although
she herself was hit by five bullets, she
successfully played dead, and while the
church building was burning, managed
to get away and hide in the grass nearby
until nightfall. Hers is the only authentic eyewitness account of what hap-

pened in Oradour; the other survivors
were not in town on that day.

Unlike the similar massacre of
Lidice, Czechoslovakia, which also
happened on a June 10th but two years
earlier and in which 192 people were
killed, the events at Oradour were kept
a secret and hardly publicized. To this
day, very few people outside France
even know about it. But, perhaps even
more sad, not enough people come to
visit this dead piece of living history,
victim of war's strange arithmetic.

39

THE POSTMAN'S

YES, ANOTHER CASTLE. Some-one up there must like castles. Perhaps that is why there are so many in Europe. But don't go away. . . .

The craziest castle-builder of this crazy, crazy, crazy world would never have dared to put up a castle like the one here at Hauterives, a half hour's drive south of Vienne. However much it looks as though it came from the imaginative cartoon brush of Walt Disney, the semi-mini castle was born in the mind of a humble letter carrier who, working in his spare time, took thirty-three years to build it.

Situated in a high-walled garden, down a side road stemming from Hauterives' main street, *Le Palais Idéal*, as the postman's castle is known, is a melange of towers and tunnels, of gargoyles and statues, of stone grotesqueries and cement bizarrenesses, of weird colonnades and screwball turrets, jumbled all together in some kind of mad-as-a-hatter plan that, like Topsy, just grew and grew and grew.

Though everyone criticized the project as it was being built and registered sheer horror after it was finished in 1912, avant-garde artists in recent years have acclaimed it as a work of sheer genius. Three years ago, the French government, wondering what the fuss was all about, took a hard look at the preposterous palace and, *sacre bleu!*, declared it a national monument.

So *Le Palais Idéal* remains today as a permanent memorial to Ferdinand Cheval. Ironically, he had hoped to be buried in his *château fantastique* but instead he lies in the village cemetery in an ornate tomb that he patterned on a smaller scale after his dream castle. There is no inscription on Monsieur Cheval's grave, but the castle carries his epitaph, his last message, which he cut into the east facade. It reads: "Life Is a Swift and Losing Race But My Thoughts Will Endure with This Place."

And he was right—judging by the number of French tourists who make the trip to Hauterives just to visit Cheval's strange piece of architecture. Watched over by two caretakers, Robert Rebattet and his wife, the grounds are open seven days a week all day long until sundown.

Cheval's dream started with a stumble. One day, while making his usual postal tour, he tripped over a stone. He picked up the stone when he noted it

Postman's Castle at Hauterives.

CRAZY CASTLE

had a curious shape and plunked it to the bottom of his sack. The next day, finding a few more stones of unusual formation, he took these home, too. For many years Cheval collected odd-looking stones whenever he came across them on his rounds. In time he filled a wheelbarrow.

A daydreamer, Cheval had always wanted to build a fairyland palace—one that would far surpass anything ever fancied in the minds of men. When enough stones had accumulated, he decided to go ahead with his dream castle, using his collected treasures as the basis to give his creation its unusual appearance. As the years passed, the unfinished castle became a passion. Sacrificing all other pleasures, Cheval spent a third of his salary every

month to buy cement and lime. Altogether he purchased some four thousand sacks of cement, not to mention hundreds of stone blocks needed to give body to the architectural mishmash.

The villagers laughed at his enterprise, as did his relatives and friends. So he built a protective wall to hide it. Cheval was entirely alone during the twenty years needed to finish the east face. As he put it, in one of the many messages he carved on the castle walls: "I could have spent my free time hunting, fishing, playing billiards. But I preferred above everything the realization of my dream."

On reaching his mid-sixties, Cheval figured that he would not have much time left. Thus, having finished the east facade, he set about furiously to complete the rest. The west face took him only six years and, consequently, it is a bit less complicated and a bit more geometrical. The two ends and the interior passageway sponged up another seven years. By then, he was pushing eighty and practically unable to do any more work. That was in 1912; he died in 1924.

Tourists who come to visit Cheval's castle, which is about thirty yards in length, can amble through the caves and archways and climb to their hearts' content among the turrets and towers. Everywhere—but everywhere—Cheval has left behind messages and comments, chipped into the cement blocks. To gladden the heart of any mailman, many people who come here get the message—and think Cheval's post-impressionist monument is letter-perfect.

CEMETERY AND TOP TOURIST ATTRACTION

GASP! When a travel guide has to recommend a cemetery as one of Paris' top tourist attractions, then we have the makings of a grave situation. Except for a few ghosts who rustle their ectoplasm, the Père Lachaise cemetery does not remind you of a graveyard—it is more an open-air museum that qualifies for the three-star rating it gets in the French *Guide Bleu*, which also gives it an unheard of seventeen pages of description.

After you have done the usual Paris visiting fireman rounds and have an afternoon to do as you please, hie yourself to a residential section in the east end of the city where you will find the Père Lachaise. Besides being a place where you can unwind, it offers tree-shaded charm with a different view of history. It has more famous people buried in it than Washington's Arlington Cemetery or London's Westminster Abbey. Covering nearly 280 acres, the Père Lachaise is something like a private park where the local inhabitants come to bask in the greenery, enjoy the cool air and perhaps relax in a shady nook. No Frenchman is ever thinking of death at the Père Lachaise when he goes for a Sunday stroll and a bit of peace and tranquility. Nor do lovers sitting on a stone bench worry about ghosts.

Most of the famous personalities buried in the Père Lachaise are in marked sectors devoted to painters, musicians, writers, statesmen and so on. In the section allocated to painters lie such famed artists as Modigliani, Delacroix, Géricault, Corot, David, Ingres, Seurat and Daumier. Not very far away are the composers, who include Bizet, Rossini, Cherubini, Poulenc and Chopin. Unexplainably, the Chopin memorial is the big drawing-card, for it seems that more hand-printed signs and chalked arrows showing the way to the Polish composer's grave are to be found than for anyone else. Among the writers in this Parisian resting place are Oscar Wilde, Gertrude Stein, Balzac, Proust and Colette for whom there are distinctive monuments and statues. Strangely enough, in the theatrical sector, there are many stones in honor of actresses but very few for actors.

What makes a walking tour of the unique cemetery such a delight are some of the graves that tell stories. For instance, there is the bas-relief to Lavalette which depicts his prison escape with the aid of his wife who exchanged clothes with him. General Labédoyère's monument tells how he was shot for having made a big fuss over Napoleon on his return from the Island of Elba.

Then there is the tomb of the painter, Pierre Prud'hon, and nearby is the tomb of a woman who loved him so much she committed suicide. At the grave of songstress Edith Piaf, a fan of hers has left behind a poem pinned to the array of fresh and plastic flowers which says: "To my little Edith—who could have thought, who would have suspected that for you a day of glory was reserved. . . ."

Some of the graves raise certain questions left unexplained. There is the grave, for example, of one Emile Courchevel who was born in 1719 and who died in 1866, giving him a life-span of 147 years! Then there is a certain

Madame Blanchard, who died in 1918; she is described as an "aeronaut." One of the oddest circumstances is that there is a grave for Victor Hugo's father but none for Victor Hugo himself. In memory of a forgotten consul of a long time ago, there is an upside-down ice cream cone about forty feet high, in contrast to the Sarah Bernhardt stone which is a small granite block with just her name and dates on it.

A number of the monuments were done by famous sculptors, some of whom now themselves lie buried in the Père Lachaise. Gustave Doré did a bust of an actress, Rodin a bust of René Piault, Jacob Epstein a bust for the tomb of Oscar Wilde, Oudine for painter Hippolyte Flandrin, Boucher for Barbedienne and D'Angers a bronze for Balzac. Getting lost in the Père Lachaise is very easy. However, any one of the fifty guards/guides who double as gardeners will give you a free map of the grounds. But trying to get un-lost is part of the fun because along the way you are likely to run across Heloise and Abelard, Adelina Patti, Isadora Duncan and Cyrano de Bergerac.

Unlike all other cemeteries, the Père Lachaise is not dead to the world, for it is indeed one of Paris' most lively spots.

*Chopin monument
in Père Lachaise Cemetery,
Paris.*

A BOOKSTORE TO END ALL BOOKSTORES

YOU CAN'T JUDGE A BOOK by its cover and neither can you judge a bookshop by its window. That brings up the subject of the most unlikely bookstore and bookseller anywhere: a Paris bookstore called "Shakespeare and Company" and a bookseller named George Whitman who prefers that people don't buy his books and who gives free lodging and food to any traveler without the price of a hotel room.

Directly opposite Notre Dame Cathedral at 37 Rue de la Bûcherie, Whitman's disarming book haven has more than 30,000 volumes on hand, many of which are not for sale (especially those over a hundred years old), though all are available for consultation. Open from noon to midnight, seven days a week, the shop with its nineteenth century atmosphere is a daily meeting point for backpackers, tourists who are broke, poets, would-be writers and even bookworm customers who have the cash to buy as many books as they can carry.

Claiming to be the illegitimate grandson of Walt Whitman, "The Saint of Notre Dame" (as the bookseller is sometimes dubbed) has lived in Paris since 1946 when he came to study at the Sorbonne. He opened his bookstore in 1951 in what used to be an Arab grocery with the intention of making it not only a wonderland of books but also a bookshop unique in the history of the book business. He succeeded. His store is never empty.

With its three stories, thirteen rooms, eleven book-lined beds and book-crammed mini-kitchen, the tumbledown mart provides a warm nook in the winter to hang out and talk and a cool hiding place in the summer to hang out and talk. In a magazine article, Whitman once said he wanted his store to be a "refuge for poets and strangers lost in the crowd . . . for those who are thirsty for the unexpected."

Asking nothing in return for either lodging or the meals he serves, Whitman prefers to do his own cooking for all guests. On any given day you can expect the standard fare of cheese soufflé, cornmeal muffins and his own unique, homemade peach ice cream "that tastes like real peaches, because only real peaches and no artificial additives are used." Another Whitman specialty is his 4:00 p.m. tea, which he serves to anyone on the premises at the time.

Downstairs, in the cellar, Whitman keeps an old press, the same one that was used to put out the first printing of James Joyce's *Ulysses*. One of his goals is to revive The Paris Magazine, a literary journal published in one edition in October 1967. Copies of that issue are today an item collectors seek and Whitman, keeping the remaining supply under lock and key, will sell you one only if he thinks you are a book-freak.

Whitman's oasis came by its name through his friendship with and admiration of Sylvia Beach who had become during the 1920s and 1930s a Paris magnet for English-language writers (F. Scott Fitzgerald, Sherwood Anderson, Ernest Hemingway, Ezra Pound and James Joyce). Her bookshop was called Shakespeare and Company and, after her death and on the occasion of the fortieth anniversary of Will Shakespeare's death in 1964, Whitman changed the name of his house of books

HAKESPEARE AND COMPAN

ПАРИКМАХЕРСКАЯ

to hers.

Since then, Shakespeare and Company has attracted another generation of big-name literary luminaries, such as James Jones, Allen Ginsberg, Langston Hughes, Lawrence Durrell, Gregory Corso and Richard Wright, not to mention hosts of other lesser-known writers who come to talk literature, exchange gossip and complaints, meet book devotees and commune with the legendary George Whitman, who lives and breathes and talks books, books, books, morning, noon and night eight days a week.

Sad to report, however, the bony Bostonian does not always have it his way in the City of Light, for the authorities have from time to time looked askance at an American selling books in competition with Frenchmen selling books. Though occasionally he is condemned

Bearded George Whitman stands in front of his Paris bookstore to chat with a writer.

by Paris courts for "engaging in an illegal business," Whitman fights back tooth and nail and supports his enterprise, whenever banned, by running a "lending library" or setting up poetry reading afternoons, literary courses and debates and seminars on great England and American books. Since the French both hate and admire his guts, he somehow manages to hang in there. Short of *la guillotine*, Whitman will not let French bureaucrats close the books on him.

George Whitman, in a Paris that is often nonchalantly philosophical, is indeed one for the books. His lifestyle speaks volumes!

A TOWN CALLED Y

ATTENTION all editors, here's the first ever report from Y about Y. The first ever report from *where*?

Y is a town here in France which has the kind of name you're likely to find in a crossword puzzle. With a name like Y (which would be hard to misspell, even if you spelled it backwards), this village near the banks of the Somme River has the distinction of having the shortest name in Europe—and perhaps in the whole world.

Y would even make old Etaoin Shrdlu, the linotyper's best friend, turn green with envy. Phonetically a loner, Y is a kind of distant orthographic relative of that place in North Wales which until recently had fifty-eight letters in its name (count 'em): Llanfairpwllgwyngyllgogerychwyrndro-bwllllanytsiliogogogoch.

Several years ago the Welsh town changed its name to Llanfair, which brought on a high-decible volume of squawks and flak. So the name was changed to Llanfairpwllgwyngyll, dropping thirty-eight of the original letters. No such thing has happened in Y because the people who live here are quite satisfied to live in a village called Y—which in French is pronounced "ee-grec." That would be six letters and a hyphen just to pronounce Y, which looks smaller than it sounds.

Mayor François Delacour of Y stands before road sign leading into his town.

And what is somebody who comes from Y called? Well, the natives here prefer to call themselves *les Ypsiloniens* or *les Yaciens*. People in surrounding regions often refer to Y residents as *Yroquois, Yennes* or *Yxiloniens*. Some English-speaking wiseacres even go so far as to call them "Y"diots, but that is likely to earn you a good swift kick in the shins if you try it here. One thing you're not supposed to do in Y, *parbleu*, is to make jokes about Y.

This comes at you quite strong when you talk with François Delacour, who has been mayor of Y since 1946. A farmer by profession and a hearty, robust sixty-nine years old, Mayor Delacour has explored all possible channels to find out how and why Y got its name. He even wrote to President Charles deGaulle back in the fifties but never got an answer.

"My own guess," explains His Honor in a most halting English, as he clutches a worn French-English mini-dictionary, "is that the name stems from a sign once put up, about three hundred years ago, to indicate a fork in the road, which looks like a Y. Somehow, because the symbol resembled a letter, we became known as Y. The name has stuck."

It's apparent that Mayor Delacour has done his homework regarding short names to be found on the map. Here in France, he cites the towns of Oo in the Pyrenees and Wy near Guiry-Vexin. And in Switzerland he has found such names as Au, Gy, Lü and Ob on the map. In Germany, according to Delacour, there are four different towns called Au and one called Oy. Norway has Al, Bo and Ed, Finland has Ii, and Iraq has Ur. But Mayor Delacour up to now has found no town on any map which has just one letter as its name. He welcomes such information from readers who know geography better than he does.

By the way, the Mayor happens to know a family living a few miles from Y which has the name of O, the shortest surname in France. He refuses to speculate on the implications and complications were the O family ever to move to Y.

Y is not a tourist town in any sense of the word. But if you're a bit weary of visiting French cities with wall-to-wall tourists and where there's a McDonald's just down the *rue*, you might do something nutty and come to Y. Mayor Delacour will welcome you and will issue a duly-stamped certificate signed by him and notarized at Le Mairie de Y, attesting to the fact that on such and such a date you visited the Commune de Y par Matigny, Department de La Somme, Arrondissement de Péronne, Canton de Ham, République Francaise.

In Y there are no hotels, no restaurants, no snack bars, no gift shops, no souvenir stands, no postcards, no sidewalks and just about no to everything else a tourist expects when he travels. There are 108 persons living in Y, most of whom make their living either as farmers or pork butchers. The only church in town is Saint Anne, shut tight on the Sunday morning I visited.

To get to Y, drive north from Paris on the *autoroute* (superhighway) towards Lille. Best get off at the exit for Péronne, and follow Highway D937 south to Matigny where you pick up the D-34 that goes directly into Y. If you'd like that stamped certificate from the Mayor, his big house is on the east side of the D-34 (his phone numbers are 81.08.10 and 81.08.08).

Y is a nice place to visit—but don't ask me wh-Y.

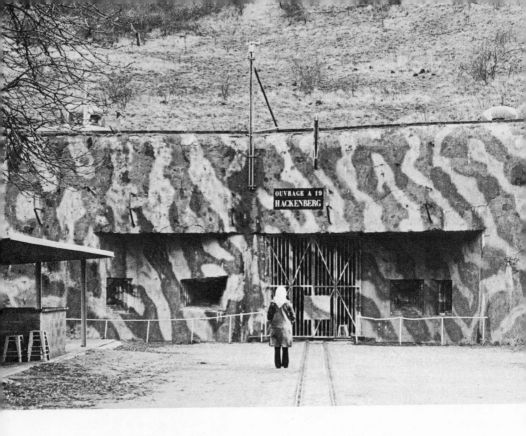

INSIDE THE MAGINOT LINE

CONCERNING the latest wrinkle in tourism, are you ready for this? The Maginot Line! Yes, folks, the Maginot Line. . . .

No, it was never destroyed by Germany, and no, it has not disintegrated into ruins. In the same solid shape it was before the fall of France in 1940, the Maginot Line is now a tourist attraction that you can visit, both inside and outside, riding on a mini-train that will take you four kilometers through its fabulous interior in three hours.

Here in the tiny town of Veckring, about an hour's drive south of Luxembourg, a few miles east of Thionville, there are guided tours into the bowels of the Maginot at the fortress called "Le Hackenberg" several times a week—Wednesday, Saturday and Sunday afternoons before 3:00 p.m. when the last indoor electric train chugs off (admission: ten francs). Bookings are made, however, only on Tuesdays and Fridays, with the Veckring mayor between 5:00 and 6:30 p.m. by calling his office at (87) 83.55.08—a bit cumbersome, perhaps, but easily arranged if done through your hotel concierge or travel agent.

The Hackenberg portion of the Maginot has the distinction of having been inspected during the war by Sir Winston Churchill, King George VI and the Sultan of Morocco. In its day, staffed by 1,100 men and forty-three officers, the Hackenberg extended for ten kilometers under 1.6 million square meters of scrubby woods, had two entrances/exits and boasted seventeen heavy artillery firing outlets. It was the Maginot's biggest unit and could truly be called an underground city, with enough electric power for a town of 10,000.

Over five hundred million prewar dollars went into the building of the famed fort which consisted of a chain of buried fortresses along the Franco-German border. Before the outbreak of the war, the Maginot Line, named after Defense Minister André Maginot, was hailed as the ultimate in defensive warfare.

Then, after Nazi tanks got behind the line by flanking it on the north and staying out of reach of its guns, the celebrated fortification became obsolete. Believing they had been betrayed by the concrete white elephant, the French people dismissed it from their minds. In recent years, however, portions of the Maginot were put up for sale, and buyers have converted them into summer houses.

Although the Maginot indeed became antiquated by subsequent warfare standards, France kept a staff of technicians and soldiers on duty for about fifteen years in nearly a hundred of the fortresses along the 250-mile stretch from Belgium to Switzerland.

"The capitulation of the Maginot line was no fault of the installation," your guide sternly informs you as the train snail-paces along through kitchens, gun emplacements, dormitories, food-storage cells, recreation halls, and a veritable anthill of tunnels, elevators, watchtowers, power plants and underground facilities for water and sewage. "If the Maginot had been continued for another mere 175 miles to the North Sea and the mobile reserve manpower supporting it had not been withdrawn, the enemy would not have been able to get behind the Line."

When visiting the interior of the Maginot, whose concrete is thicker than any existing fortification or castle, you will find two heating systems, one for winter and one for summer, but take a warm wrap with you because it's quite cold underground.

Equally fascinating are the precautions against flame throwers and poison gas. The ventilation intakes, for example, pass the air through two hundred feet of pebbles before being forced into charcoal filters the size of a bass drum. And the Line's interior pressure could be raised higher than the outside air pressure to prevent poison gas from seeping in.

When the guide turns on any faucet, fresh clear water comes up from the deep wells inside the fortress. Flipping a switch here and there, your tour leader will set in motion diesel generators, AC-DC converters and other electrical gear. The elevators can take you up in some places as many as twelve stories. The living quarters, bunks, kitchens, chapel, hospital, storerooms, toilets, shower rooms and zig-zag tunnels amaze any blasé tourist who's been "everywhere and seen everything!"

The Maginot is one attraction that will rank high—number one on the best cellar list.

49

THE CARDBOARD TOWN

IT IS ALL A GIGANTIC FAKE—the phoney fishermen's cottages, the make-believe medieval frontage and the ersatz terracotta roofs. You get a creepy feeling as you approach Port Grimaud on the Mediterranean coast (a bikini's throw from St. Tropez) because you know the town is just a facade, completely made out of cardboard so that camera-bugs can photograph it.

The man who conceived this utterly preposterous idea of erecting a picture postcard village where none of the buildings are real has even gone to the extent of paying women to hang out lines of washing, native-style. Anything to add to the contrived local color and to delight the lens of your visiting Leica. That's Port Grimaud, the most bogus town in all the universe. But this is precisely its charm. In 1966, it did not exist. The marsh on which it was built had been up for sale for years; nobody wanted the useless tract of land with no character to it, even though it stood geographically equidistant between famed St. Tropez and posh Ste. Maxime.

Seen from afar, Port Grimaud looks like another old port. You could never tell the difference, unless you took note that the fronts of the houses are all suspiciously clean. But with the various motorboats and sailboats moored in the harbor, you walk towards the bluff burg and do not notice such things. Besides, your camera is champing at the bit now. To help you to put a hocus-focus on the most magnificent hocus-pocus in Europe, there is a little electric gondola which creeps slow-motion along the main canal. The canal and the

"buildings" that present themselves are a hybrid mixture of Venice and an old Mediterranean fishing port, but a bonafide fisherman you'll ne'er find. So who cares?

The brains behind this very-odd-place-indeed is an architect from Mulhouse, one François Spoerry, who got the idea one day from a little model he saw in Zurich. He decided to create the same setup on a large scale, but "I wanted it to be a Mediterranean village without the clichés of modernism, a village as it would have been if architects did not exist." One thing that possessed him, however, was his determination that every house front would have its own boat outside.

Meanwhile, Spoerry has built real homes and real buildings in back of the cardboard facade. Already some nine hundred structures have gone up and they are now occupied by actual people. The work on this housing-for-real project will go on for at least another five years, at the end of which Port Grimaud (the real town behind the facade) will have a population of 10,000. Spoerry is selling homes at the equivalent of $13,000 for two rooms and $65,000 for seven rooms.

Port Grimaud is very much a one-man affair. Ruling with an iron hand and a leather thumb, Spoerry forces the present shopkeepers (whose stores were all built in advance of the rest of the town) to stay open till ten o'clock every night with all the lights lit. With the pioneer crop of inhabitants being strictly regulated as to the amount of noise they can make after dark, Spoerry takes the attitude that if anybody does

not like his system, he can get out. So far, no one has. And the waiting list to buy a Port Grimaud home or apartment gets bigger and bigger.

As far as the postcard side of the establishment is concerned, Spoerry knows that, when the word really gets around, the tourist trade will leap. Presently Port Grimaud draws a casual, half-day crowd of the curious from St. Tropez ("Even Bardot came down to look us over one day!") and this is about the size of its peekaboo traffic. But there are a hotel and a restaurant for tourists who want to tarry longer.

It's all a cardboard front
at Port Grimaud.

For all his efforts, Spoerry has not been without his share of enemies. Some two thousand infuriated members of the League Urbaine et Rurale are dead set against the "instant antique," which they have dubbed "Spoerry's toy for the eye." They charge him with building an outright deception. Which he candidly admits Port Grimaud is.

51

AN ONION MARKET

THIS CAPITAL CITY of the world's oldest democracy is the only place in the world that sets aside one special day for the most democratic of all vegetables—the lowly onion, which, like garlic, has a smelly reputation.

Berne's love affair with the little bulb, a tearjerker, goes back to May of 1405, when three-quarters of the city was burned by fire. Though all the nearby towns sent token aid, Fribourg provided over a hundred men to help clean out the charred ruins. Grateful for the aid, the Berne city council granted Fribourgers the right "for all time and eternity" to hold a market here. Inasmuch as the onion constituted the main product of that region, a special market was set up for it. A real sight to see is the Swiss Parliament building, just before the sales begin, knee-high with onions piled in white, yellow and red mounds.

That day—the fourth Monday of November—is now an important feast day in Berne. The country people come to town dressed in their picturesque national costumes and the streets are filled with tourists, onion buyers and students gaily masquerading as onions marching in procession to one tavern after another to make merry. The day has become known as *"Zibele Marit"* (the "Onion Market") and housewives take the occasion to stock up on the bulbous vegetable for the entire year, until the new harvest comes around. The women braid the onions into strings and hang them in a cold, dry place, the better to lop one off when needed. Another custom that prevails in Berne and environs is the invasion of the bedroom of a newly married couple to bring them a huge tureen of piping hot *soupe à l'oignon gratinée*. The Bernese believe that this onion soup not only has great restorative qualities and brings warmth on a chill night but also is a marvelous aphrodisiac.

Because the onion is king in Berne, it is possible to go into a restaurant and order a meal devoted entirely to it. For instance, you can start with onion soup, follow that up with roast sausages stuffed with onions, coupled with a side

dish of liver and onions, mix in a heap-
ing plate of onion salad and a healthy
portion of fried onion rings, and top it
all off with a Berne specialty, onion
cake. For the kiddies, local confection-
ers even make a candy in the form of a
small onion, flavored ever so faintly
with an onion taste. At the come-hither
delicacy stands, one can also get hot,
aromatic, bite-size onion pies, with
rich crusts crinkled to a perfect shade of
brown, yum!

"We grow three kinds in Switzerland," explains a friendly farmer
around whom pervades the unmistaka-
ble odor of the halitosis vegetable. "We
have the pungent, the sweet and the
mild flat types. Also, we grow the very
small kind which we Swiss use for pick-
ling. It's easy to recognize a good onion
when shopping. The good ones are
solid to the touch, bright and shiny with
dry crackly skins. The onions you
should reject are the ones with moist
necks or bristling sprouts. In peeling ᴜᴇ
onions, you can save a lot of sweat and
tears by peeling them under cold water.
The small ones can be dunked into hot
water, boiled for a minute and then
rinsed with cold water. They'll peel
very easily without the slightest trace of
odor—and no tears."

That the onion contains one of the
most powerful germ killers in the
world, according to the farmer, is borne
out by the fact that scientists tested the
bacteria-killing power of 150 plants and
found the onion to be the most effective. If one chews a raw onion, he ar-
gues, it will sterilize the mouth and
throat and even, in many cases, cure a
cold. Onion juice mixed with water

and glycerine also makes an effective
gargle.

Weighing up a forty-pound sack for a
customer, the farmer completes the
transaction and continues his conversation. "*Allium cepa*, that's the onion's
real name. Its ancestry goes back to
prehistoric times, to Central Asia and it
was the principal diet of the slaves who
built the Egyptian pyramids," he adds
matter-of-factly. "Did you know that
the onion is a member of the lily
family?"

One thing you can say for the Bernese. They certainly know their onions.

THOSE SWISS BUSES

SOONER OR LATER, it's bound to happen to a tourist in Switzerland. Innocently, he gets on one of those Swiss buses—and the rest is history.

Swiss youngsters don't aspire to become president of their country when they grow up. No! As far as every kid in Switzerland is concerned, the ultimate number one success in life is to make it

*Swiss bus approaches
one of the many hairpin turns
along the famous Furka Pass*
(PHOTO BY IRENE ROONEY LO BELLO).

as a driver for one of the country's postal buses. Around here, if you have such a job, you are considered the luckiest chap on the planet.

Because this work is deemed the most glamorous in Switzerland, thousands of men apply each year but only a handful make the grade. And one of the keenest satisfactions for those who become big wheels in the postal service is to be shown a letter of praise, invariably from a foreign visitor, who reports he will never, but never, forget watching his bus driver "attack" the spine-tingling exorbitant turns of Helvetia through peaks ever so lofty and plateaus ever so undulating.

Every year, Switzerland's postal buses carry about fifteen million passengers, some half of whom are tourists. Though the primary purpose is to transport the mail over more than four thousand miles of Alpine challenge, the buses also pick up passengers going the same way. Running on 200 to 250 horsepower engines, the canary yellow vehicles have jointed front axles for taking sharp turns. But, to be on the safe side, there are three separate braking systems, each of which can do the job alone. Small wonder that, since World War I when the postal bus system started up, the drivers have not had one single fatal accident—and mighty few minor incidents, to boot.

Swiss bus drivers are unbelievable. With skills that are matched nowhere else, these mountain jockeys take their four-wheeled dinosaurs over all manner of improbable highways to time-lost villages, some of which are five thousand or ten thousand feet up. To them, a road hugging the side of a mountain that has no guardrail separating you from a drop of several thousand feet is duck soup.

To qualify as a driver for the Swiss post office, an applicant must be no older than twenty-eight, have had at least four years experience as a mechanic and one year as a truck driver, have completed his military duty and be able to speak three languages. Having met these requirements, plus a stringent physical exam, he goes into training.

Assigned initially to a postal truck for several years, he then runs a postal bus in the lowlands until he is ready for an exam that would scare the bejeebers out of anybody—literally a baptism of tire. The final test consists of driving up a narrow mountain road just about wide enough for a bus to fit. About two thirds of the way up, the candidate is told to go halfway back in reverse and then make a U-turn.

This absurd about-face, made at a two-by-four landing, usually takes some seventy maneuvers before it can be negotiated. Notwithstanding, the examiners see to it that the would-be chauffeur has to make it with a bus full of veteran postal drivers who heckle him every inch of the way. If he makes it without plunging into the gorge, he passes the exam.

A tourist who goes for a ride on a Swiss postal bus will never forget it. For the end-most in travel-thrills, select a trip that takes you over the most difficult summit in all Switzerland, the Furka Pass. This impossible mountain top requires special driving techniques inasmuch as the driver has to cope with hairpin turns that are diabolically sharp and follow each other, one right after another, through the clouds.

You will be tingled by the crackerjack operator in the pilot's seat up front whose handling of the steering wheel can best be described as ultra-feverish. According to local custom, if your driver gets you over the Furka alive (which is always), the passengers usually burst out into a round of applause.

Another thing you will get a bang out of is the horn, for on every blind turn the skipper will honk to warn oncoming traffic. This will always bring a smile because the horn's notes are from Rossini's "William Tell Overture"—and you know what that did to the Lone Ranger.

A ride on a Swiss bus, therefore, is a good way to put into high gear a vacation that may have hit the skids. Try it. This is no bum steer.

THE MINI-EST MINI-STATE

THE OLD SAW THAT "you have to see it to believe it" really holds true for S.M.O.M., the smallest country in the world. It takes a couple of good looks to believe what you see and then you come away still not believing that this Tom Thumb empire measures in total area about the size of two tennis courts.

Where in the world would you find a country like S.M.O.M., which is over 920 years old, which has a population of eighty and an Air Force of fifty planes? The answer is: downtown Rome, along the Via Condotti, about a three-minute stroll from the American Express office.

Tourists hardly ever hear about S.M.O.M., otherwise, many of them would not miss a chance to get their passports stamped by the mini-est mini-state of them all. S.M.O.M. issues its own passports and auto license plates, mints its own money in the form of gold and silver coins and even prints postage stamps.

A tourist crossing the border onto S.M.O.M.'s extraterratorial soil is confronted with a medieval courtyard full of automobiles, many with the S.M.O.M. license plate, red letters on white. At the far end is a gargoyle dribbling water into a pool of goldfish, above which is a red and white Maltese cross. Embracing the yard is a four-story palace which houses the private apartments of S.M.O.M. officials, legations and a hospital.

During my visit, Prince Enzo di Napoli Rampolla, the seventy-year-old Chancellor of S.M.O.M., laid aside matters of state and took me on a tour of the whole country. Here and there we passed members of the S.M.O.M. militia, stiff-looking hall guards garbed in tailcoats, who snapped to histrionic attention. Through passageways that were lined with maps, paintings, model ships and ancient tapestries, I walked into a green-bedecked conference chamber, a gold-hued hall of state for visiting ambassadors and an impressive gold and red dining salon where Prince Rainier and Princess Grace attended a state dinner not long ago.

Founded in the year 1048, before the First Crusade, S.M.O.M. has managed to hold on to its sovereignty, even though some contemporary countries like Slavonia, Catalonia and Lower Lorraine have long since passed on. At various times during its seesaw history, S.M.O.M. has been located on the islands of Rhodes, Malta, Cyprus and Sicily. Transferring to Rome in 1834, it settled at Number 68 Via Condotti, next door to a haberdasher, about three-hundred yards from the Spanish Steps.

Recognized by thirty-nine countries, S.M.O.M. is engaged primarily in running hospitals, clinics and nursing schools in various parts of the world. It uses its armada of planes, which are piloted by hired flyers from Italy, for evacuation and rescue work during times of catastrophe and war.

Currently S.M.O.M., which is the official abbreviation for Sovrano Internazionale Militare Ordine di Malta (The Sovereign International Military Order of Malta) maintained (without a smidgin of publicity) ten "white cross" teams in Vietnam. These unarmed, four-man squads provided medical treatment to Vietnamese children injured by Viet Cong mines or American bombs. As part of its foreign hospital program, the state also administers three leper colonies in Africa, dozens of dispensaries in Western Europe, hospitals all over Italy and crackerjack ambulance corps in four countries.

Perhaps the oddest S.M.O.M. possession is a keyhole—the delight of many a tourist. Through it, you can view an extraordinary panorama. On top of Rome's historic Aventine hill, S.M.O.M. owns a villa which is not open to visitors. But if you peek through the keyhole in the door of the high-walled garden, you can see the entire dome of St. Peter's basilica, perfectly framed, in the distance.

"We have a man on duty whose job it is to clean the fluff out of that keyhole every day," Prince Enzo says. "We are indeed proud of that keyhole. It is the only keyhole in the world through which you can view three countries at the same time—Italy, Vatican City and S.M.O.M."

Famous scene through the keyhole.

THE BAMBINO
OF ROME

NEARLY 1,500 CHRISTMAS letters from all parts of the globe descend every December onto "The Bambino," a two-foot wooden doll kept in a chapel of the Church of Santa Maria in Aracoeli, bearing such cryptic addresses as "The Baby, Rome"; "Enfant Jesus, Autel du Premier Né, Rome"; or "An den Bambino, Rom."

A bejeweled figure of the Christ Child, The Bambino is probably the world's most famous Christmas doll. In recent years, children have taken to dispatching telegrams and even cables in the hope that the cherub-faced Bambino might give them special attention.

The letters that pour in are stacked at the feet of The Bambino, after being

Statue of the Bambino
and some of the letters sent him.

checked for valuables or money. When the Christmas season is over, they are then taken away and officially burned. No letter is ever acknowledged or returned.

Sometimes, while envelopes are being opened, a particular note catches the eye of a church inspector. Several years ago, for example, one kiddie communication caused a chuckle among the priests and nuns. Writing from Venice, a seven-year-old girl said:

"Dear Bambino, my mother is awaiting a baby. So make him healthy, make him intelligent and make him obey me."

No official explanation exists as to how the custom of sending Christmas letters to The Bambino ever took hold. The practice started early in the eighteenth century and, after a few stories were printed in Italy and abroad, The Bambino's "fan mail" from nearly every country grew to heavy proportions.

Consequently, each year a number of requests reach the church from stamp collectors asking for the privilege of sorting the envelopes before they are burned. One stateside collector even went so far as to imply he was writing on behalf of President Franklin D. Roosevelt, whose philatelic collection had had considerable publicity at the time.

According to one historian, everything about Italy's most famous doll is mixed with fact and fiction. Said to have started out as an olive tree in the Garden of Gethsemane, the doll was reportedly carved by a Franciscan monk from the tree trunk into the image of the Christ Child and baptized in the River Jordan.

In the latter half of the 15th Century, The Bambino was supposed to have made his way towards Rome to join the rest of the Holy Family in the life-sized manger scene being assembled at the Aracoeli church. En route, The Bambino's ship met some severe weather and he was cast overboard in his handmade trunk.

The chest floated with the currents for a few weeks and at last reached Italy, supposedly just in time for the Christmas pageant at Aracoeli. From the very beginning, The Bambino fared well and, by popular demand, was baptized the second time. On May 2, 1897, Pope Leo XIII crowned him King of Rome.

During a Christmas show once, a childless widow is said to have kidnapped The Bambino and taken him home. One version of the tale, no doubt exaggerated by Roman storytellers over the years, claims that The Bambino left his hostess under his own power, climbed the 124 steps to the Aracoeli church, rang the bell to get in and put himself back in his old roost.

Once, during the height of Italy's Fascist period, The Bambino was being driven in an automobile by some clergymen for a sick call somewhere in the city. While passing Piazza Venezia where Dictator Mussolini was haranguing a huge turnout of citizens, The Bambino virtually stole the show from the big-jawed dictator. The crowds turned their attention away from the balcony and pushed to take a peek inside the car at another celebrity.

One unidentified wag is said to have remarked at the time: "Italy has more respect for the wooden doll than for that wooden head in the balcony."

CURIOSITIES

OF THE ETERNAL CITY

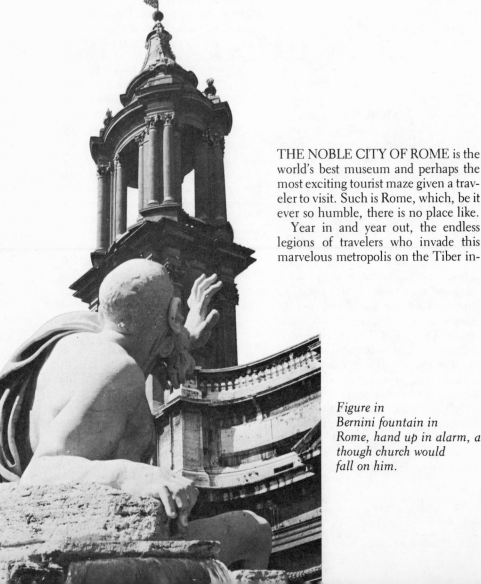

THE NOBLE CITY OF ROME is the world's best museum and perhaps the most exciting tourist maze given a traveler to visit. Such is Rome, which, be it ever so humble, there is no place like.

Year in and year out, the endless legions of travelers who invade this marvelous metropolis on the Tiber in-

Figure in Bernini fountain in Rome, hand up in alarm, as though church would fall on him.

variably manage to cheat themselves of visiting some of the Eternal City's art oddities. So, suppose we put our guided chairborne missile into an Urbi-et-orbit tour and inspect Rome's curiosities.

The Fountain of Trevi, star of the film, "Three Coins in the Fountain," may well be the most famous fountain in the world. Lesser known to the million visitors who come during the summer months is the episode between builder Nicola Salvi and the barber who had his shop in the red building nearby.

While the fountain was being put together, the barber, irked at the disorder and the piles of stone, kept making complaints from his doorway about having to "look at that ugly thing in my mirror all day long." To show his contempt, Salvi erected a huge slab of marble on the right side of the fountain; this was hewn into the form of a big vase, which, according to the artist's intention, represented a barber's lather-bowl and blocked the barber's view of the art. That odd bowl is still there, but most Trevi visitors rarely even notice it.

One of the most intriguing of all art curiosities is right at St. Peter's Square. People who visit the Vatican *piazza* and admire Bernini's imposing colonnade of 284 Doric columns and pillars are not usually aware of one of the sculptor's sly touches, namely the cobblestone on which you stand. If you stand on the right one, your view of the columns is such that you can see only the first row. The other rows disappear, giving the impression there is only one set of columns all around.

A half hour's walk away, at Piazza Navona, stands another structure with a story behind it. Bernini's gigantic Fountain of Rivers. History tells us Bernini despised Francesco Borromini,

the designer of the Church of St. Agnes opposite the fountain. As a deliberate insult to Borromini, sculptor Bernini made one of the statues in the fountain group cover his eyes with a hand so as not to have to look at the church. Then, adding injury to this snub, Bernini carved another figure with hands up in alarm, to make it appear he was afraid the church would fall down upon him.

Inside the Church of St. Peter-in-Chains, you will find Michelangelo's statue of Moses. Not generally known is that the slight scar on the statue's right knee was made by Michelangelo, who threw his mallet at Moses, shouting: "Why don't you speak?" Unknown also to most visitors are the profiles of Pope Julius II and Michelangelo himself, cleverly hidden in Moses' flowing beard. It is a kind of optical illusion— so you have to look hard for this one.

In one of Rome's handsomest palaces, the Farnesina, is to be found a unique art curio. When Raphael was painting at the Farnesina, he was so jealous of his work he forbade anyone to see it. One day when he had to go out, he gave strict orders to the watchman to allow no one in.

Burning with curiosity to see what his rival was up to, Michelangelo disguised himself as a peddler of beans, slipped past the unsuspecting guard and observed Raphael's unfinished work. With a piece of charcoal, he made a hand sketch on one of the walls of the Galatea Room. After Raphael returned, he took one look at the drawing and exclaimed: "This is Michelangelo's doing."

Though miffed, he left the sketch there. Today, it is considered the most valuable visiting card in the world.

THE NOON CANNON

YOU CAN'T JUDGE a city by its noise pollution. But Rome may be the exception, judging from the way most tourists here have to go through thick and din to find a little quiet. Though saddled with the unofficial but dubious honor of being the capital with the highest decibel count, the ear-splitting Eternal City boasts an unusual tourist lure that—hold on to your eardrums!—is *fortissimo*, louder than loud.

A few hundred people make the trek daily up to the top of Janiculum Hill where Garibaldi and his magnificent bronze horse overlook the city, to be there at noon precisely. With their penchant for doing everything in the loudest possible way, the Romans fire a cannon each day at twelve o'clock sharp so that everybody all over town can set his watch or clock with the correct time.

The midday gun is one of Rome's odder sights and it warrants a visit. Rain or shine, that fieldpiece makes its diurnal BOOM when the clock strikes twelve. Come a bit early if you want to get an advantageous spot along the wall so that you can look down at the whole show.

A squad of six Italian soldiers wheels the old weapon out of its brick-lined cave and onto a wooden platform out front. Under the direction of Warrant Officer Mirello Brilli, the gun is loaded with about two pounds of explosive. When everything has been checked, Salvatore Ausilio, a civilian specialist in artillery repairs, takes his place at the trigger, ready for the command signal from Officer Brilli.

At 11:45, Brilli gets a phone call from City Hall, whereupon he reports that the cannon has been greased, primed, wheeled into place, and that everything is ready. At three minutes before twelve, the telephone rings again and now the countdown begins, as a red light is beamed from a tower at City Hall—just in case the telephone is cut off.

Brilli stays on the phone and listens to the recited numbers. At fifteen seconds before noon, he raises his right arm and Ausilio comes to attention. At four seconds, Brilli holds up four fingers and lowers a finger each second. At precisely twelve o'clock, the count reaches zero, the red beam goes out and Brilli's arm swoops histrionically. Ausilio instantly pulls the lanyard, and the cannon fires. Windows rattle for at least a half mile away (occasionally one breaks), and the puff of smoke covers Janiculum like floating whipped cream.

Initiated in 1847 by Pope Pius IX, then ruler of Rome, the noon cannon shot came about because a huge timepiece on the Quirinal Palace, then the home of the Popes, only showed six hours to the day. A Swiss Guard official one day remarked to the Pope that he could not understand a clock that pointed to four but rang ten times to indicate the time was twenty-two hours. Perhaps the Pope couldn't understand this any more than you or I can so Pius ordered the first noontime shot to be fired on December 1 to serve as a standard for all of the twelve-hour clocks in the city.

During the Second World War the practice was suspended, but in 1959 an

Janiculum cannon.

Italian comedian, Mario Riva—then emcee for a popular television program, *Il Musichiere*—started a campaign to get the cannon back. Thus was the noon gun blast revived.

Because the Pope's original cannon was no longer available, another cannon was put on duty. Curiously, it had never seen any war service. Made in 1918, the cannon is a Hungarian one and bears the serial number 149 M14/16 #1115(1918)24484P. Affectionately known by an unprintable Italian slang nickname, the revered gun, which came to Italy as war booty, will one day be placed on permanent view in a museum.

Only twice since 1959 has "Old Faithful" ever given trouble. By mistake, a double charge of powder was once placed into it and the resounding clap that followed broke windows all over town. Another time, the gun got wet during a heavy rainstorm and failed to go off. City Hall was swamped that day with hundreds of calls asking what happened.

Despite the precision of the beloved noonday cannon, most Romans nevertheless go on being late for all their appointments anyway. Yet no one can say that Rome does not like to do things with a bang.

THE UNDERGROUND BONE MUSEUM
ON VIA VENETO

IN THE ROMAN DEN of antiquity, with its more than 450 churches, you would have a hard time pinning a label on which could be classified the most unusual church of all. Yet right on the famed Via Veneto, a stone's throw from Federico Fellini's haunts, is a church that comprises one of the least-known but most fascinating attractions in all the Eternal City.

It is, however, a good place to stay away from, some say.

On the other hand, if you are not easily frightened and are eager to tackle travel curiosities, then follow me to the seventeenth-century church of Santa Maria della Concezione. Make sure your wife has her smelling salts tucked away, as we walk down Via Veneto past the deluxe hotels, past the American Embassy, past the elegant shops and past the busy night clubs to a little-noticed ramp of steps on the left hand side of the street.

At first glance, the structure does not look like a church. Inside the place, which is also known as the church of the Capuchin Monks, you will encounter a painting of St. Francis by Caravaggio and another by Guido Reni of St. Michael fighting the Devil. But the shock attraction of the church is downstairs in the basement, where there exists a strange collection that is over a hundred years old.

In its own way, it is a "work of art" that contains the bones of over four thousand monks who died between the years of 1528 and 1870. In the subterranean corridor, which is broken up into six arched compartments, stands an assortment of human bones that

have been artistically arranged in eye-arresting tableaux of clever designs and patterns.

You do not easily forget what you see. Arrayed across the ceiling and arches, and along the walls of each chamber, are hard-to-believe figurations of loose tibias and "fibias". Shin bones support lamps that flicker, collar bones wreathe ribs, and skulls and vertebrae form skillful cross designs. The layouts look like floral arrangements.

Among the bones there are also the remains of famous Italian personages, like Prince Matteo Orsini (great-grandson of Pope Sistus V), a very young princess, a Patriarch of Jerusalem and several of the papal Zouaves who fell in the Battle of Porta Pia in 1870. The soil in which these individuals are buried was brought over from Jerusalem by Pope Urbanus VIII in the early seventeenth century.

"We do not get too many visitors coming here," explains bald-headed Fra Costante, custodian of the underground collection. "But those who do are invariably touched by the marvelous pictorial arrangements, the decorative motifs and the graceful lines which bring to mind the drama of the end of life. Indeed, in a cumulative way it invites prayer and meditation."

The effect of the hooded skeletons in their various standing and recumbent poses is often unpredictable. Actually a half dozen women a month who have dared to enter the underground "bone museum" manage to faint away. For such occasions, the dark-robed custodian on constant duty at the foot of the stairs is well supplied with smelling salts and a dark brown medicinal fluid that will corral any wooziness.

Just who created the fantastic osseous masterpiece is unknown. According to Padre Ireneo, who is the *superiore* of the forty-five Capuchin monks administering the odd cemetery, the work is believed to have been conceived and carried out by a French friar.

Exuding a sinister grace, several of the macabre settings were seen in an Italian movie starring Princess Ira Furstenberg. She spent a week shooting among the crypts and never once came close to fainting. In fact, she was rather impressed with it all, since it evoked in her a feeling of awe rather than of horror.

The quick and the dead are very close in the arty downstairs graveyard, and no contrast of life and death will ever be more evident to anyone who is a bug on history and would like to do a bit of boning up.

Museum curator prays at one of the Bone Museum exhibits
(PHOTO BY JIMMY BEDFORD).

THE HOLY STAIRS

AS WITH OTHER open-air museums, Rome is hard on the feet. This multifaceted metropolis has such a profusion of sights to offer that whether a tourist sets aside five days or five weeks, he could ever so easily overlook many guidebook footnotes.

One such "footnote" is the Holy Stairs, which were transported from Jerusalem by Emperor Constantine's mother (later St. Helena) in the year 335 A.D. Every day, hundreds of believers ascend the twenty-eight steps of the unusual stairway on their knees, a sight that never fails to touch a visitor, whether religious or not.

During Easter Week, the Holy Stairs (*Scala Santa*) are crowded from morning till night. But no matter what time of the year you get there, dozens of kneeling figures are to be seen slowly working their way up the steps saying a prayer on each one. Custom requires that anybody who starts the upward climb (on his knees) is obliged to continue to the top, lest he offend the other worshippers present.

Only one person is known not to have done this. That was Martin Luther. According to a thoroughly authenticated account, he was halfway up the stairs when he suddenly got off his knees and walked back down to the bottom. Roman Catholic officials have never debunked any aspect of the stairway's history, though the Vatican is vigilant about negating unsubstantiated stories.

The twenty-eight steps of Tyrian marble, which today are protected by wooden boards, at one time were in the residence of Pontius Pilate when he was governor of Jerusalem. Jesus went up and down these steps on the day Pilate condemned Him to death, and the glass-covered bloodstains on some of the steps are supposedly those of Christ.

After being brought to Rome, the stairs were placed in the Lateran Patriarchate, and for hundreds of years they were called *Scala Pilati* ("Pilate's Stairs"). In the late sixteenth century Pope Sisto V had the flight of steps placed in a building across the street, facing the basilica of St. John Lateran.

Considered one of the most cherished mementos of the passion of Christ, the staircase became known as the Holy Stairs. From the very first day of installation, the faithful have climbed the steps only on their knees. Each step requires a special brief prayer, printed copies of which can be borrowed free or acquired at the desk to the right of the entrance for a small offering.

Pope Pius IX, on the night of September 20, 1870, a famous night in Catholic history, left his old home in the Quirinal Palace for the last time and was driven to the Holy Stairs, there to ascend on his knees. Italian troops had marched into Rome, ending the temporal power of the Pontiff and, from the top of the stairway, Pius sadly blessed his supporters before imprisoning himself inside the Vatican. He never again left it.

At the top of the Holy Stairs is the ancient Palatine Chapel of Popes, called the *Sancta Sanctorum*. This is the Sistine Chapel of the Middle Ages, but it is open to the public only a few times in the year—though the chapel can be viewed through a massive iron grating when closed.

With frescoes from painters of the Cimabue and Perugino schools, the unusual chapel, which at one time served as a secret archive for the Church's most precious documents, houses a large number of relics of martyrs and saints. It also contains the highly revered "Acheropita Image" of Christ, an oriental icon painted on a walnut board that was used for worship during the late Middle Ages.

To walk down there are two corresponding staircases on either side of the Holy Stairs. Visiting the *Scala Santa*, a tourist who wants to see all of what Rome has to offer comes away with the feeling that the Holy Stairs is one footnote that is best seen step by step.

THE TALKING STATUE OF ROME

DID YOU EVER HEAR A "talking statue"?

Well, Rome has one—but one with a pretty bad reputation, enough to have made some big shots gnash their teeth. Called by the name of Pasquino, the weather-beaten marble torso has a most fascinating history that has rescued it from the humdrum of a museum.

Pasquino stands behind the Braschi Palace, just off historic Piazza Navona, on the corner of Via di S. Pantaleo. Most tourists pass him by without a second look and you can hardly blame them, for Pasquino's delectable charm is not for the eye at all. What "talking statue" is?

Originally a Greek work from the third century B.C., brought to the Eternal City to grace the reception salon of some Roman luminary, Pasquino literally came up from the mud in the year 1501 to sling mud at the city's politicians, the clergy and the aristocracy. The statue had been buried up to its neck outside the shop of a hunchbacked tailor called Pasquino, whence the name, and his customers had been using the top of the head as a stepping-stone to cross the muddy street.

Signor Pasquino the tailor drew customers to his place by the hundreds, thanks to his sharp wisecracks aimed against the establishment. After the tailor's death, his home was razed and the statue that had been used as a stepping-stone outside his door ended up on a pedestal. Now a strange transformation took place.

The old battered statue took on the name of the outspoken tailor—and inherited his loose Will Rogers tongue. In an epoch when speaking your honest opinion was not what you would call conducive to good health, Pasquino the statue began to criticize the government and just about everybody else who needed a dressing down.

Pasquino poked fun at the church. Pasquino held the government up to ridicule. Pasquino shot off his mouth about taxes. Pasquino decried the phonies in power. And, being a true citizen of Rome, he exercised a fantastic sense of humor. His criticisms were acid because he liked to make his digs with needle-sharp epigrams and cutting puns. Nothing escaped Pasquino's fine-honed sense of humor and his irreverent tongue which hurled sarcastic splinters where they hurt the most. Today many of Pasquino's witticisms have become part of Italy's speech.

For instance, when the Barberini Pope, Urban VIII, was stripping Rome's ancient monuments for materials to be used in building his own palace, Pasquino had a famous comment: "What the barbarians did not do, the Barberinis did!"

Of course, it must be said that Pasquino the statue was only the medium through which Romans, suffering under a system where there was no freedom of speech, cleverly said their piece by sneaking, under cover of darkness, to the statue and pasting their anonymous messages to it. These were called "pasquinades." And the next day, everybody in town would ask with a twinkle, "Did you hear what Pasquino said last night?"

Why the pestiferous Pasquino was not torn down, only the silent historian

Pasquino, "the talking statue"
(PHOTO BY SIMONETTA CALZA-BINI).

could explain. But suffice to say, Pasquino stuck around through the centuries. The authorities tried to stop Pasquino in other ways, such as the decree of 1727 which said: "Whosoever writes, prints, distributes and publishes libels of the 'pasquinade' type, even if these state plain truths, will be punished by death and confiscation of property."

But Pasquino merely chuckled up his marble sleeve. And kept on.

Perhaps Pasquino's most famous pun is the one he made during Napoleon's occupation of Rome. Punned Pasquino: *"Son tutti ladri questi francesi? Non tutti, ma Buonaparte si!"* ("Are these Frenchmen all thieves? Not all, but a good part are!") "Buonaparte" (literally translated as "a good part") was Napoleon Bonaparte's name before he Frenchified it from the original Corsican form.

After his mockery of the Fascist era, Pasquino has not been heard from in a long time. That is not to say, however, that Pasquino won't be ready with his back talk when the right time comes. For Rome, Pasquino will always remain the talk of the town.

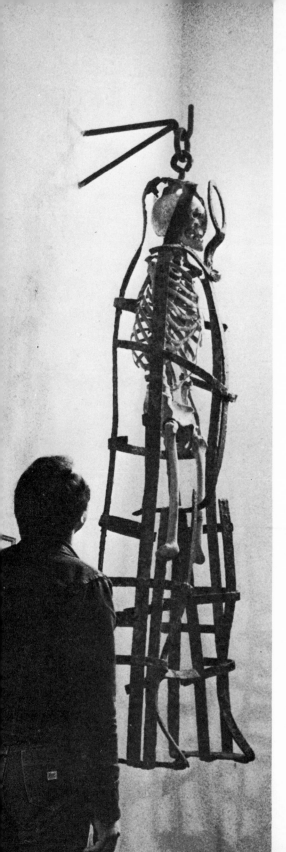

Skeleton in torture device in the Criminal Museum.

ROME'S
HOUSE OF HORROR

AGAINST A BACKDROP of ancient ruins and Renaissance settings, the imperishable Italian capital, draping a toga end over its left shoulder, sometimes gives visitors the impression that it has a zillion museums. Whether true or not, there is one Roman gallery from which people stay away in droves—and it may well be the least-visited museum in all Europe.

This is the Criminal Museum of Rome, more descriptively called the "House of Horror." Open only on Sunday mornings from nine to twelve, the collection draws an average weekly attendance of fewer than ten people. Housing some of Europe's most fantastic exhibits, the museum nevertheless is the kind of place most persons go to only once, forthwith advising their friends to shun it at all costs "because you've got to have a pretty strong stomach to walk around that place."

Opened in 1930 by decree of the Italian government, the Criminal Museum is intended primarily as an educational device. For one thing, every rookie policeman in training is required to visit the premises and study the various exhibits on which later he must take a written examination.

Because common decency does not permit description of some of the items, we will skip over the more offensive aspects of the Museum and look into some other showcases. One salon, for instance, that immediately captures attention, after you have wandered through the "Suicide Chamber" and the "Homicide Chamber," is the "Capital Punishment Chamber." Apart from showing in morbid detail, through wax figurines, the various methods used both past and present, of executing offenders throughout the world, this room displays what may well be the largest collection of guillotines (most of them blood-stained), gathered from various parts of the Italian peninsula.

As you rove your way past handcuffs and leg irons of every variety, bullwhips and cat-o'-nine-tails, thumbscrews and other diabolical torture devices, you run smack into the skeleton of a woman chained to the stone-blocks of a dungeon wall. Condemned to die of hunger and thirst two hundred years ago, the victim was found in 1933 in the castle of Poggio Catina exactly the way you see her in the Museum. Nearby is an iron cage in the shape of a human being, inside of which are the original bones of the prisoner who perished in it.

The Museum, which is housed at Via Giulia 52 in a building put up in 1655 by Pope Innocent X, also has on display a number of curiosities the police have picked up in the course of duty. These include the diamond ring worn by Sicily's Robin Hood bandit; a collection of illegal tattoos; prison escape contrivances of every imaginable kind, including a real-looking gun made out of bread crumbs; the brain and punctured skull of the would-be assassin of King Umberto I; some personal effects of Mussolini's mistress, who was machine-gunned and publicly hanged upside down with the murdered Duce.

Also blackmail letters received by Italian big shots; some heavy iron safes, blown open; soap bars and candles made by a murderess from the bodies of her three victims; counterfeit stamps, medals and money; forged paintings and sculptures of famous originals; a pair of snowshoes that leave the tracks of an animal; ingenious dope-carrying containers; confiscated pornography; and a startling collection of art made by criminally insane inmates (one oil depicts the crucified Christ as being the Devil with horns).

Not long ago, one of the Museum's alert guards detained a visitor who acted in a suspicious manner. He kept returning to the same case which showed a body of a murdered woman and staring at it with bulgy eyes. Further questioning led to a check in the police files and it was learned that the gendarmes of another country had a warrant out for his arrest.

The Criminal Museum of Rome truly gives one the creeps—but apparently it does not keep some creeps out.

71

THE BOMARZO GARDEN OF MONSTERS

A CHAMBER OF HORRORS in stone . . . a Kafkaesque garden theatre of statuary monsters . . . a weed-tangled menagerie of sculptured gargantuas . . . a bestiarium of baffling brutes and behemoths . . . a terrifying nightmare in dried volcanic lava. . . .

This is Ogre Garden!

With its mysterious enclosure of freaks—a half acre of satan-like ogres, which are both spine-chilling and staggering—one can understand why Bomarzo's Garden of Monsters gives the heeby-jeebies to most tourists. This spooky place, sixty miles north of Rome, brings every visitor face to face with the oddest array of bizarre statues this side of Boris Karloff.

A few years ago, England's Princess Margaret spent half a day visiting what is perhaps touristdom's most frightening attraction, the Villa Orsini, in an Etruscan-haunted valley of Italy's central mountains. She exhaled a sigh of relief when she finally walked away.

Another illustrious visitor, painter Salvador Dali, made an offer to buy the statues, no price limit, but the Italian government declined. When he came to study the extraordinary sculpture, Dali delighted the locals by posing in the six-foot mouth of one of the Brobdingnagian faces. That particular megalosaur, twenty feet in height, is supposed to represent the mouth of Hell leading to Pluto's cave. Rimming the leviathan lips is the sentence: "You Who Enter, Leave Behind Every Thought."

Though it may not have been Princess Margaret's cup of tea and, despite its having been grist for the Dali mill, you will find the Villa Orsini a place

you cannot forget. If there are indeed proverbial faces that would stop a clock, Bomarzo's collection is guaranteed to start all cameras.

Since the sixteenth century the grotesque forms—figures of dragons, animals, pagan gods and satyrs, all carved from volcanic tufa—have confounded Italians living nearby. Until recently the origin of this surrealist park of horrors was unknown. Research by European art specialists finally brought out some of the story of Ogre Garden. The statues were built at the behest of Duke Pierfrancesco Orsini in 1572 by Turkish prisoners-of-war captured in the Battle of Lepanto. Designed by Giacomo da Vignola, who succeeded Michelangelo as the architect in charge of St. Peter's Basilica, the strange limestone figures were supposed to serve as a memorial to the Duke's dead wife. Orsini had wanted the sculpture to convey the impression of a sacred pagan grove.

The two sphinxes that stand guard at the gateway, for instance, appear to be giving fair warning to all who enter. Inside, you immediately confront an elephant with a castle on his back crushing a gladiator in his trunk. Nineteen feet tall, the elephant is a symbol of Eleazar's slaying of the beast of King Antiochus, whose attempt to wipe out Judaism brought on the rising of the Maccabees.

Giving it some close competition for horror honors is a dragon doing battle with a lioness for the possession of her cubs, one of which lies crushed beneath the intruder. Half-concealed behind a nearby rock stands a huge Hercules, with thighs like tree trunks, sav-

One of Ogre Garden's spectacular monsters.

agely tearing an upside down young human figure to pieces.

Nearby is a huge fighting dragon, from a Leonardo da Vinci sketch, engaged in a death struggle with two lions. Further away squats an eighteen-foot reproduction of King Neptune with one of his snake-like marine companions. Alongside a slope rests the most forbidding of all the creations, a ghastly sub-human face which is half sunk into the earth and which bears a cracked globe of the world on its head.

The eerie premises have been pre-served in several movie sequences and even immortalized in an opera. Impressed with the Renaissance collection of uglifications, Argentine composer Alberto Ginastera wrote an opera called, "Bomarzo," based on the garden and the hunchbacked Duke of Bomarzo.

Admission to Ogre Garden is free, thank goodness. Otherwise, there would be the devil to pay.

73

THE
PURGATORY MUSEUM

THOUGH NO GUIDE BOOK mentions it, the Purgatory Museum —which very few people have ever heard of—houses a collection of "things" that make it the world's eeriest museum. The so-called "things" which, once seen, are never forgotten, comprise a collection of "proof that

Mark of a left hand next to a crude cross, both burned into wood, possibly the most important relic in the Purgatory Museum.

some people have returned to earth from the beyond."

Known also as the House of Shadows, the Purgatory Museum displays some pieces of charred cloth, a painting, several photographs, a plank of wood and a few old prayer books. Each of these has a reason for being in the unusual array, for each bears the print of a hand or finger burned into the surface by "some soul who came back from purgatory asking for prayers that

would release him into paradise."

Although the museum was built with the encouragement of Popes Pius X and Benedict XV, the Vatican today remains steadfastly silent about the "signs from those who return." Yet each of the "things" on exhibit is there because its history has been thoroughly documented, according to the curator, Father Ernesto Ricasoli. The visitor must decide for himself what to believe or disbelieve.

For instance, there is the burned hand print of Madame Leleux on her son's sleeve which dates back to June 21, 1789. Dead twenty-seven years, she appeared in front of her son and begged him to change his sinful ways. Before she left, she touched his sleeve so as to convince him of her visitation. After the apparition, the son converted to a life of Christian principles, founded a new religious order and lived out his days in a pious and charitable way.

In another documented case, the apparition of a young woman's mother-in-law, who had been dead for three decades, asked the woman, Margherita Demmerle, to make a pilgrimage and have two masses said for her. After having carried out the dead woman's request, Margherita was then revisited by the apparition who reported that she had at last been liberated from Purgatory. As the mother-in-law was about to depart, Margherita asked for a sign to prove her authenticity. Placing a trembling hand on a nearby open prayer book, the visitor burned a deep hole through some of the pages. That was in the year 1814, and the prayer book with the tell-tale fingerprints is now on permanent display in the Purgatory Museum.

Perhaps the most important relic in the museum is the mark of a left hand next to a crude cross, both burned into wood. Originally this was the top of a work table owned by Mother Chiara Isabella Fornari, prioress of the Clarisse Sisters of Todi. On the night of November 1, 1731, the nun received a visit from the dead Abbot of Mantova, a Father Panzini. Though the details of the conversation between the priest and the nun were never given, she did report that Father Panzini left several signs of his presence by drawing a cross with his finger and leaving his left hand print on the table.

"The assortment in the Purgatory Museum was started by Father Vittore Jouet toward the end of the nineteenth century, and he traveled widely to amass quite a large collection of 'things' " explains Curator Ricasoli. "The museum remained open until 1920 when his successor, Father Gilla Gremigni, decided to reorganize the exhibit and eliminate all but the most thoroughly authentic pieces. The museum stayed closed for thirty years and, when it reopened, only a small number of 'things' has survived penetrating inquiry."

Today all the remaining exhibits are on display in a large cupboard in the annex of the Sacro Cuore del Suffragio church, which flanks the Tiber River and is located on the Lungotevere Prati, within eye-view of Rome's skyline landmark, the Castel Sant'Angelo. There is no sign or arrow to indicate the museum, so visitors must ring the sacristy bell and ask the custodian for the *Museo del Purgatorio*.

Silently he will lead you into a dark corridor and then into a small, windowless room—but not until you have stepped a few steps down a small stairway. Which may or may not be a coincidence. . . .

Cupola in the great Church of St. Ignazio draws tourists to it because the church has no cupola (PHOTO BY SIMONETTA CALZA-BINI).

THE CUPOLA THAT ISN'T

TOURISTS DO NOT like to be deceived. But Rome has one great illusion which deceives all tourists—and everybody loves it. It is the "cupola that isn't," which some people call the "cupola that never was."

But, whatever you call it, the cupola in the great church of St. Ignazio draws tourists to it because the church has no cupola. Yet 999 people out of a thousand who look up at the central nave of the magnificent seventeenth century church will swear that there is one there.

There really is not that much mystery, however. Simply put, the St. Ignazio church has no cupola but the flat canvas painting up there gives the impression there is one. The painting, which is believed to be the biggest in Rome and one of the largest in the world, stretches across the nave as one of the truly unique examples of three-dimensional art anywhere. When you look at it, you believe you are seeing a cupola soaring up, built on eight columns, with sunlight pouring through the circular opening at the top. No matter from which angle you examine it, it appears to be a beautiful cupola. It is very difficult to believe that what you are looking at is nothing more than a flat surface.

The "cupola that isn't" has a fascinating history.

Back in 1684, when the church was almost completed, plans for a dome were abandoned because the Dominican fathers at a nearby church protested it would block out their light in the library. To resolve the dilemma, the builders called upon the great master of perspective of the eighteenth century, Andrea Pozzo.

Pozzo studied the situation and promised to create a deception whereby a cupola could be simulated by perspective techniques on the flat ceiling. Using a round canvas that measured fifty-four feet in diameter, Pozzo painted a make-believe cupola and raised it 108 feet to the ceiling. His portrayal of St. Ignatius Loyola (who brought Christianity to India) gave it the reputation for being the finest cupola in any Roman church. It fooled people for centuries; even guidebooks referred to it as an outstanding example of a cupola.

In April 1891, a violent windstorm tore the canvas and it was covered up to hide the damage. Over the decades, the great piece of illusionary architecture was practically forgotten, except by the art experts. Even new editions of tourist guidebooks dropped any mention of the incredible art accomplishment. In 1961, with the help of Rome's fire department, restoration of the lost "dome" began. A huge 150,000-pound steel frame hoisted to the ceiling enabled the lowering of the "cupola" to the ground. The workers then discovered that what had hurt the painting was not so much the wind as it was the load of dirt and soot, over 560 pounds of it, which had accumulated atop it for more than two centuries and which had been bearing down on it.

Headed by Professor Pico Cellini, art experts had to work two years to make repairs and restore the painting to its original brilliant colors. Then, in 1963, the "cupola that never was" was hoisted back into place with the use of sixteen winches and twenty-three firemen.

The church of St. Ignazio is not on the usual tourist circuit—a pity, indeed. To reach it, you must follow the Via Caravita off the busy Via del Corso west towards the Pantheon. The best spot to view the artistic curiosity is from a circle marked on the floor. The "cupola that isn't" commands everyone's admiration and awe, once one finds out about it. Small wonder then that many people look up to it.

SHANGRI-LA IN THE ALPS

"SHANGRI-LA in the Italian Alps!"

By all standard rules of logic, the town of Gurro—easily the strangest of all Italian villages—should not be in Italy. The people here speak French better than they do Italian, but whichever they speak, it comes out with a Scottish brogue.

For the oddball thing about this oft-forgotten clan of Italian citizens is that they are the descendents of war-weary Highland mercenaries who settled in this hidden hilltop corner nearly 450 years ago. Not until after 1900 did Italian government officials come to learn that; for some four centuries, Gurro lay dormant in its snowbound Alp haven, a veritable Celtic Shangri-La that had all the earmarks of a Rip Van Winkle story written by Sir Walter Scott.

Nearly all of the 725 residents of Gurro are direct descendants of the Scottish soldiers who discovered this remote perch near the Swiss frontier, a half-hour drive from Lake Maggiore near the border town of Cannobio. You reach Gurro after following a twisty, uphill, narrow mountainside road that is paved with potholes, big stones, ruts and, in rainy weather, gobs of mud. What is scary about the road is when your auto meets a car or truck coming downhill and it is, according to the unwritten rules of the region, your obligation to go backwards until the road widens.

Anthropologists from Zurich University were the first to come across Gurro. Since then, Swiss philologists have had a field day recording the hundreds of non-Italian words the locals still retain in their dialect from Gaelic, which resembles no other language in the zone. Altogether, there are about

78

eight hundred Scottish words in their language. To cite one curiosity: the word "meh," which means "not" in Scotch. Although Italians usually put their "not" (written "non") in front of the verb, the Gurro folks put theirs after.

"As to how our Scot forebears settled here, the story is that the stragglers of a regiment of Scottish archers, salaried bodyguards to King Francis I of France, who invaded Italy in the early half of the sixteenth century and was defeated in the Battle of Pavia, fled north with the idea of finding their way back to safety in France," explains schoolteacher Antonio Dresti (the family name is a derivative of Desmond).

"That was the year 1525, and the snows were especially heavy. So the Scottish archers, unable to combat the snow and knowing the Simplon Pass would be blocked, decided to pause at the high point that is now Gurro and hold out. Left to their own devices in hostile country, the hundred Scot troops figured they would be able to make their way home."

Apparently nobody bothered to give chase. So the runaway soldiers simply stayed on after the spring thaw, partly because the location smacked of their own Highland glens and partly because it would be easy to defend. Like the *Bounty* mutineers, the Scots eventually took local wives by "raiding" the nearby mountain villages and forthwith built a mountain fortress community that is the Gurro of today, 2,657 feet above sea level.

Today, the heirs of these original Scotsmen live in a kind of utopian peace and harmony, hardly bothered by the outside world or, for that matter, by the rest of Italy. With nary a police-man in Gurro, because there is no need for one, about the only "crime" that ever gets committed around here is the loud singing of a happy imbiber at midnight.

The occasional visitor who does drift into this ethnic enclave finds the Scot-Italians quite friendly. Quick to inform you that the kilt is no longer worn by the males and that the women hardly wear their plaids anymore, they also tell you that, because of economic reasons, most of the able-bodied men have to go to Switzerland to find jobs.

Living in Gurro are a surprising number of old-timers, pensioned-off Americans who left here as children and who have come back to live out their retirement years. Though they love their Shangri-La, they lament nevertheless over the nearby mountain-top transmitter that relays the television shows from Rome and Switzerland. The thing manages to get itself de-stroyed by lightning about once a month.

One little old lady with a basket of hay slung across her shoulders was asked to pose for a photo. After the snapshot was taken, she inquired: "Will I be on television?"

Anachronisms, anybody?

Main square of the town of Gurro.

BOLOGNA'S

TWO LEANING TOWERS

STEP ASIDE, PISA. Bologna has *two* leaning towers! No point in beating around the bush—tourists are hereby alerted that the leaning towers of this arcaded old city have as high an eye-Q as their illustrious cousin in Pisa.

Though both of the towers are neither taller nor more bent than Pisa's, the Torre degli Asinelli and the Torre Garisenda are just as old. They have not been the beneficiaries of press agent puffery, yet the crooked edifices provide a new slant that cannot be equaled even by Pisa's.

It goes like this: Bologna's pair of passed-up perpendiculars are so close to each other that, if you stand at a certain place (more about that later), the angle gives the impression that the two are kissing each other!

Perhaps one of the reasons Bologna's two tipping towers never made it in the big time of touristdom is that both of them are ugly ducklings in comparison to Pisa's white-marbled structure. But, unlike the Pisa attraction, you can walk to the top of the Asinelli tower (486 steps) and get a marvelous view of the city.

Built of pebbles, cement and mini-bricks by the Asinelli family between 1109 and 1119, the slender tower, 320 feet high, was at one time taller than the Pisa tower, but its top was chopped off because it had begun to lean, a process that has since stopped. Today it is about four feet off center—a fact that is not immediately noticeable to the eye because the lean of the nearby Garisenda tower is more obvious.

Tilting ten and a half feet towards the northeast, the Garisenda, which was also built in the twelfth century by a family that was in political cahoots with the Asinelli clan, is only 158 feet high. Work on the Garisenda had to be curtailed because the soft earth underneath brought about a lean that made the engineers worry it would fall down. In fact, during the fourteenth century, thirty-nine feet had to be lopped off to save it.

Like the thousands of other towers in Italy, the Asinelli and the Garisenda were erected as combination fortresses and homes by noble families. The owners would usually live on the lower floors but would retreat to the upper stories, blocking up the narrow winding stairways, when danger presented itself in the form of a military attack.

Some of Italy's towers which are over two hundred feet were made taller and taller over the centuries because many a rich family just could not tolerate another neighbor's fortress-home over-looking their own. Besides, it was a kind of medieval status symbol for an influential family to have the tallest tower in town, and to this end no expense would be spared.

Bologna's two towers were built so well, despite a poor choice of location where the base did not allow for great height, that they have outlived several big fires, a number of direct lightning bolts and other sundry damages. So much did Dante admire them that he sang their praises in a well-known passage of his *Divine Comedy*. Even Charles Dickens saw fit to make public mention of them when he said: "Look at them bow to each other, stiff and strange!"

To get the best view of Bologna's strange lovebirds (not counting some fine helicopter photos on postcards) go directly to the center of town in the part known as old Bologna and, at Porta Ravegnana Square, which is an outlet for seven main streets, stand on Via San Vitale about five yards from the corner of Via Luigi Zamboni.

The neglected leaning towers are not very far from the city's other main attraction, the University of Bologna, the oldest university in the world, founded in the year 425. Standing literally in the shadow of that estimable seat of education, the Asinelli and the Garisenda towers give proof that a little leaning is not a dangerous thing.

A FAKE TOWN IN NORTH ITALY

THIS TOWN [Pop.: 650] is a genuine fake.

Although nearly every structure in the tiny hamlet of Grazzano Visconti is strictly pseudo, it is, paradoxically, the only make-believe town in Europe that is for real. The buildings are thirteenth century, but they were built about fifty years ago as a result of one man's dream.

Visit this village—reconstructed as a hobby according to medieval architecture and principles—and you almost get the feeling that Snow White and the Seven Dwarfs will come dancing through one of the portals singing "Whistle While You Work."

However, make no mistake about it, Grazzano Visconti is a real town. People reside here, work here, raise their children here, live entire lives here. In spite of any first impressions this place conveys, it was not put up as a tourist attraction per se, having been born because a man had an idiosyncratic yen to build an actual village in the style of the Middle Ages.

Behind the creation and development of Grazzano Visconti was the late Count Giuseppe Visconti, who in 1919 had inherited a large parcel of land from his father. Once having restored the family castle, which dated back to the year 1390, Count Visconti figured he would design a village to go with it—but a village with real inhabitants, who would do the kind of work for a living, such as furniture-making and iron-forging, that the artisans of long ago used to do, trades that have virtually disappeared in our time.

Though the castle is closed to the public because it is the private home of a branch of the Visconti family, the rest of the town is yours to ogle and admire. Walk through the castle gates and you enter the Square of the Weeping Willow, which leads to the main street.

Now you see the post office, the town barber shop (with its set of old-fashioned soap mugs) and the metal-working foundry where the village smith, naked to the waist, and his boy apprentice fashion their wrought-iron magic into take-me-home objects. You are plunked back to the thirteenth century, with wall-to-wall history.

A stone's throw away is the Biscione Hotel (itself the very model of a medieval inn), where you can book lodgings for the night. Painted on the hotel's facade is Count Visconti's family motto (which reads: "Olta. ni. ad. raug. e. eneta. pipmi"). If you cannot make any sense out of it, that's because it is printed backwards, but the translation says: "Be indifferent and look at the sky."

Though Grazzano Visconti was not intended for tourism, the town has become quite an attraction, especially for Italian visitors who travel from all over to inspect this unique reconstruction. About three hundred people a day come here during the warm summer weather, and most of them tarry long enough to have a meal at the Hotel Biscione in one of the two large dining salons. When the weather is good (which is often), the hotel will set up rows of tables outside on the street, where you dine with the pleasant scent of wood in your nostrils.

One thing that is a must-do-at-any-

Main square of town of Grazzano Visconti.

cost here, especially if you are a student of the cinema and an admirer of Italian director Luchino Visconti, is to view the two paintings which depict him as Christ. It seems that Count Visconti, besides planning and building the town, also had a penchant for painting, especially Madonna and Child scenes with members of his family as models. Luchino Visconti was used twice as the Christ Child.

One of the paintings hangs in the main square and depicts Luchino not only as the angelic Infant Christ, but also as a rather devilish young man kneeling behind his father and gazing adoringly at his own image. The other Madonna and Child (Visconti again) hangs in the small chapel on the main street next to the nursery school.

If you happen to come to Grazzano Visconti on a Sunday, there is a special treat awaiting you, for all the women and girls, including some cute toddlers, dress in medieval costumes. Somehow or other, it strikes you as the proper window dressing for the most different of all villages, a stage setting of an epoch gone by.

To get to Grazzano Visconti, you leave twentieth-century Milan and drive a mere forty-eight miles right into the thirteenth century.

THE TRACKLESS RAILROAD STATION

EVER HEAR OF A one-and-only tourist attraction that everybody is ashamed of, that nobody wants to talk about?

That the city fathers keep behind barbed wire. . . .

That never gets mentioned in the guide books or plugged by the travel writers. . . .

That even Mr. Ripley did not know about—believe it or not?

Savona, on Italy's Ligurian coast,

View of Savona's
trackless railroad station
(PHOTO BY IRENE ROONEY LO BELLO).

about 30 miles northwest of Genoa, is not the kind of town that ordinarily agitates the tourist barometer. It is a charming, bread-and-butter city, whose busy port handles a volume of four million tons of traffic a year, consisting mostly of coal and oil. In essence, it is a mini-edition of Genoa sans

84

the spectre of Christopher Columbus.

So not many tourists pop in, and who can blame them? But wait a minute, Mr. Travel Buff! There are two plusses to chalk up for Savona. There is, for one thing, the Pancaldo Tower erected in memory of the sailor from Savona who was Magellan's pilot in his voyage around the world. And then, for another thing, there is Savona's dazzling railroad station—the one with no tracks and no trains.

Savona's trackless railroad station took seven years to construct and was completed in the Spring of 1962 at a cost of approximately one billion lire. The builder was Italy's internationally famous architect, Pier Luigi Nervi. In all the years the station has been ready, not one train has ever pulled in, nor has a single passenger passed through. Alley cats and weeds have overrun the platforms and track lanes.

But, by any standards of comparison, the station itself is without doubt today the most beautiful and most modern railroad depot in Italy—and perhaps in all Europe. Known as the Stazione Mongrifone, the structure looks like some kind of palace, all done in shiny marble, with non-skid rubber floors and artistic decorations aplenty.

There is a fully equipped, plush restaurant with seating capacity for about two hundred people, a coffee bar with an espresso machine ready for immediate action, and even a chapel with special kneeling pads for anyone who wants to pray. There is not one single item missing at the Stazione Mongrifone—except the tracks.

When you ask people in Savona about the station, they decline to say anything about what they consider their city's "brutta figura" (ugly public shame). If you ask directions how to get there, apparently nobody knows where it is. To really find out, better ask a kid, the kind you have been seeing in those Italian films over the last decades. The small fry do not seem to have any feelings of shame about yon unmentionable.

Most of the kids will even show you how to sneak in, as one tattered nine-year-old did with this writer. It is not too hard. You have but to climb a high mound of terrain, gingerly using stray broken bricks and loose stones as the steps. Although there is nothing to hold on to, except maybe the kid's shoulder, it is worth a try. The only other barrier is the barbed wire, which your little guide will help you through.

What is needed to connect Savona's trainless wonder to the rest of Italy's railway system is less than a kilometer of tracks. And therein lies one of the most incredible deadlocks in the history of Italian politics.

The foul-up is red tape, compliments of three political villains—the Italian Ministry of Public Works, the State Railroad Bureau and Savona's City Hall. Simply put, the three of them have just not been able to get together over who pays for the tracks.

Astonishingly, they cannot even agree to split the costs three ways because none will agree as to what the shares should come to, if divided among the three. The main argument, however, seems to run to the effect that each litigant wants the other two to assume the full burden, an expenditure that would come to about $250,000.

Despite the piddling amount of money involved, the squabbling politicos just cannot seem to railroad this deal through. So Savona is left with its no-track station because everyone involved has a one-track mind.

THE KISSING STATUE OF RAVENNA

WANT TO BET there is no man in all history, alive or dead, who can match Guidarello Guidarelli's record? He has been kissed by more than two million women—or is it three million now? That's pretty good for one man.

Although he has been dead for over 470 years, the kissing is still going on. Tourists by the thousands flock every month to this North Adriatic coastal town to visit the lucky Italian and plant a sincere big smack on his appreciative marble lips.

Yes. Guidarello Guidarelli is a statue. But don't go away, because there's more to the story of how a soldier killed in the sixteenth century has managed to get himself bussed by so many lovey-dovey damsels, many of them foreign travelers who come to Ravenna especially to be at his side. It's nice work if you can get it—and Guidarello Guidarelli has got it.

Somehow or other, about a century ago, the word got around among girls looking for a husband that, if you planted a kiss on the lips of the statue of Guidarello, it would bring good luck, a husband, a home and fine children.

Nobody knows how true this is, if at all, but the fact stands that up to now women of all ages from just about every country of the world have gone ga-ga over G.G.

This reporter watched one morning as several girls trekked into the Cloister of Santa Maria in Porto and, with determination, marched right up to the statue. Some of them fondled his face, or gave him a hug, or squeezed his hand, or whispered a soft word into his attentive ear. But all of them made with that unabashed peck. G.G. never blushed once. Talk about keeping a straight face!

Hewn by sculptor Tullio Lombardi at the behest of the knight's wife, Benedetta, the statue of Guidarello Guidarelli is a reclining figure in full battle armor. His war blade has been placed full length down his body and

Statue of
Guidarello Guidarelli in Ravenna.

his hands are reverently crossed over his chest and sword hilt. Realistically, his helmet is a little bit crooked because the head is tilted to the left side.

So perfectly did Sculptor Lombardi chisel out G.G.'s facial features that he looks almost alive. Having seen for themselves, many women who visit here pronounce the knight's physiognomy as the "most beautiful male face" they have ever seen.

"There is something about that face that is just adorable," admitted one Australian ex-nurse from Melbourne. "It has a magnetic and masculine force to it that is most irresistible to a woman. It has a mystic chemistry about it."

Target of so much osculation, Guidarello Guidarelli, by the end of a day, has changed hue somewhat. The reddish tint you notice by evening time is not a blush at all but accumulated lipstick traces. Every night, after the Cloister shuts its doors, custodian Domenica Schiari comes around with a piece of alcohol-soaked cotton and sponges G.G.'s face clean again.

"I've been doing it for a long time," Mrs. Schiari says, her elbow resting on the G.G. forehead. "The main part of my job, nevertheless, is to see that women do not hide themselves so they can stay with the statue after we lock up. A few manage to do so each year, but now we make a half-hour check all night long to discourage nocturnal visitations. The teen-agers are the ones you have to watch for."

As for the historical facts about Guidarelli, he was born in Ravenna and made a knight by King Federico III. Known as "Strongarm" in his day, he led a thrilling life until felled in a duel with Paolo Orsini on March 26, 1501, at the age of 33. Centuries later, Italy's great poet, Gabriele D'Annunzio, wrote an ode about him.

But the biggest honor to the marble lady-killer came from Sophia Loren. On a tourist visit to Ravenna, she too got into the act and planted a nice juicy one on G.G. Newsmen following her around that day asked how it felt to kiss a man so old. Answered Sophia (whose producer-husband Carlo Ponti has 22 years on her):

"Gentlemen, why ask such a silly question? You know I like older men!"

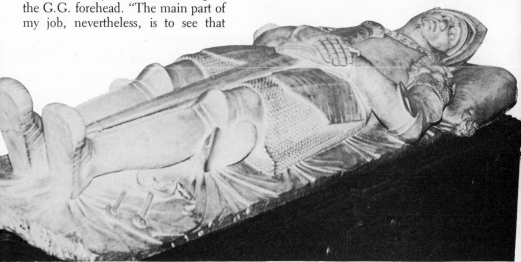

THE HAZELNUT LADY

NO TOURIST WOULD EVER come to this city to visit a cemetery, of all things. Yet the tourist guides of Genoa, without exception, take every one of their clients to the Staglieno Cemetery for what they know to be the most underrated and certainly one of the most absorbing travel sights.

Familiarly known as Genoa's "City of the Dead," the Staglieno draws more tourists each year, according to official government figures, than does the house of Columbus. Approximately two miles from downtown, the "City of the Dead," which was first opened in 1844, maintains a double, horseshoe-shaped gallery that burgeons with one work of art after another—magnificent marble scenes showing some of this port's old families.

Except for the Hazelnut Lady (of whom more later), all of the figures represent men and women from Genoa's families of yesteryear which had amassed prestige and money in trade and finance. Wanting to use some of this wealth to preserve themselves in marble, these Genoese would commission the top sculptors of their day to exalt the family name in stone with poses and settings that would touch the heart.

All this may sound a little slushy, but the statues are indeed masterpieces of Italy's neo-classical and realistic periods. So lifelike are they, you expect them to move at any moment. Composer Richard Wagner, taken to the "City of the Dead" against his will, was to write glowingly of it: "I never saw anything so beautiful as the Staglieno."

Like Wagner, the touring visitor will be impressed as he stops at each monument. There is, for instance, a grief-stricken girl, clad in a long-flowing marble robe, with a realistic tear on her cheek, as she peers under the death shroud covering her father. Down further along the main gallery, you pass a sturdy-winged boy gathering up the sail of his small boat. The artist has depicted the stormy sea of life which "can be safely crossed by the mortal who follows the path of Christ."

Soon you reach the monument dedicated to Luigi Pastorini, a surgeon. At the base of the statue is a hospital nun in her huge headgear, holding a sickly boy on her knee. Above her is an angel tilting a plate from which coins are cascading down onto the nun.

The Perelli monument shows a wavering palm tree under which a gentle girl is seated next to a tiny waterfall. She is cupping her hand and drinking some water at the behest of Christ standing nearby. Symbolically, the Pinoli family commemorates itself with a maiden, hand raised toward the sky while she stands among high reeds in a field. In the background are several dozen swallows flying off.

Perhaps the statue that attracts more attention than any other is the one the tourist guides like to save for the end. Ironically enough, the statue was erected for a peddler of hazelnuts who worked the streets of Genoa. Indeed, though she was a woman of no financial status, she has taken her place among the statuary of the rich.

What is her story?

Beloved by the Italians, who call her monument the "Campodonico," her tale is related in the long inscription chiseled into the base. The woman had worked for years in rain and sun, cold and heat, hawking hazelnuts and a kind of coffeecake on the sidewalks of Genoa to earn as many coins as she could to fulfill her one passionate goal—that of leaving a sculptured model of herself in the Staglieno for posterity.

Covered with a tassel shawl, the simple old peddler is shown with her skirt skimming the top of her large shoes. Her rustic Sunday apron is neatly pressed and, in her work-thick hands, she holds several strands of hazelnuts and two ring-shaped coffeecakes. The last line of her epitaph reads:

"If My Memorial Pleases Your Eye, Please Pray For Me In Passing By."

In her own way, the hearty peasant woman, with her rugged face and strong features, succeeds in giving today's tourist a lump-in-the-throat reminder of that anonymous philosopher's message—that every man owes a death to society.

PINOCCHIO PARK

THOUGH HE IS over ninety years old, you'd never know it. There isn't a wrinkle on that sympathetic, earnest face. Not bad for a little boy made out of wood whose nose grew bigger every time he told a fib. And now Pinocchio, hero of children everywhere, has become a tourist attraction for young and old alike.

When you visit tiny Collodi, a fetching Tuscan hamlet twenty-two miles northeast of Pisa in an area surrounded by woods and meadows, you step immediately into the storybook world of the most beloved, mischievous marionette of all time. Collodi, which was the home of Carlo Lorenzini, author of the Pinocchio stories, has erected a 25,000-square-yard Pinocchio Park "dedicated to the happiness of children everywhere."

The first thing you see, as you enter this fairy-tale haven (also called "The Land of Fables"), is a sixteen-foot bronze statue of Pinocchio looking up at the Blue Fairy and the Falcon sent to rescue him when he was "hanged" by the Assassins.

Nearby is the eye-arresting Magic Mosaic Square, whose panels—stone by stone—depict many sections of the book. At first sight, the mosaics deceive you, but tarry and look closer, for, as if by magic, you begin to detect certain sights: Geppetto whittling the block of wood, the green fisherman with the fry-ing pan, the patient snail who brought food to Pinocchio, the talking cricket, the fox and the cat at the Inn of the Red Crawfish, the three doctors, Pinocchio with the puppets Harlequin and Pulcinella, and the man who was wider than he was tall.

You will also see incidents from the little shaver's scarey misadventures before he turned into a real boy, such as the serpent who burst from laughing, the jail where Pinocchio was locked up, Geppetto inside the whale, the tree of the gold piece, the dog Alidoro who saved the runaway boy's life, the spider's web, the Fools' Trap Town, and the children of the world dancing ring-around-the-rosy.

Pinocchio Park also has a library containing more than 2,400 different editions from all over the world of the sad deeds of the splinter delinquent, including a rare copy in Latin entitled, *Pinoculus*. In the attached Fire-Eater's Theatre, the kiddies can watch marionette and film shows, and at certain times of the week actors from the Italian stage or Rome's movie colony will come to give histrionic readings from the pages of *Pinocchio*. When a Gina Lollobrigida or a Claudia Cardinale shows up to do a bit of reading, it's surprising how many fathers edge out their sons for the best seats.

Perhaps the most inviting aspect of Pinocchio Park is the Inn of the Red

Pinocchio.

Crawfish, a faithfully reconstructed family-sized Tuscan restaurant *(trattoria)*, the kind of place author Lorenzini described so well. Besides getting a good meal in the Florentine style, visitors can also stay overnight if bookings for the few rooms upstairs are made ahead of time.

Conceived by a University of Florence literature professor, one Dr. Rolando Anzilotti, Pinocchio Park was inaugurated in 1956, on the 75th anniversary of *Pinocchio*'s publication, with the help of children from everywhere who contributed small coins that surpassed a total sum of $300,000.

Although celebrities such as Elizabeth Taylor, Ingrid Bergman and Curt Jurgens have toured Pinocchio-land (British actress Diana Dors filmed some scenes for one of her movies here), Collodi town officials were especially eager to get Jimmy Durante to make a visit, because "his nose is famous, too!"

Collodi also runs an annual contest in which youngsters up to the age of 14 submit sketches (which must measure 15 by 18 inches) portraying one of the *Pinocchio* episodes. The winner gets a free ten-day trip to Collodi and, as a consolation prize, every loser receives a Pinocchio Certificate. This entitles the bearer to tell one tiny lie without his nose growing longer.

VILLA OF THE SIXTEEN FOUNTAINS

ASK ANY ITALIAN who knows his travel ABC's and he will tell you that his country is studded with quite a few tucked-away marvels that most people pass by. "The Villa of the Sixteen Fountains" in Bagnaia, a tiny medieval town near Viterbo (four miles off the main road between Rome and Florence) is one of those touristic plums that Italy somehow manages to keep to itself.

"The Villa of the Sixteen Fountains," which is officially known as Villa Lante, has in fact more than sixteen fountains. The figure is more like six hundred. Originally planned as a "water theatre," the Villa enables H_2O to play nearly a thousand different roles—not to mention a number of unexpected, thoroughly mischievous practical jokes on everybody who comes here. You won't get wet, not really, but you'll nevertheless jump here and there, every now and then, as a secret fountain or spout suddenly traps you in an artistic frame of dancing moisture.

For instance, since water here has neither a beginning nor an end, you are presented with a wet surprise the moment you walk through the gate. A hedge of water, as if by magic, suddenly mushrooms up from out of nowhere barring your way. Naturally, you stay put. Make one false step backwards or forwards and you will get soaked. You have to wait until Mr. Laughing Liquid tames itself down before it will allow you to proceed to the next playful surprise.

And that comes when you expect it least. As you start to walk up the stairway, between two of the steps (we're not telling which two!), a jet of fluid greets you in a flash, forcing you to halt your upward stroll. Or the water welcome can come as you turn down a shady lane, for all at once you are totally enmeshed in a labyrinth of overlapping streams that will stop you in your tracks. Standing apprehensively in the middle of this design, you begin to marvel as to why you are not getting one single drop on yourself, though fully surrounded and imprisoned by the bossy spray.

The hydraulic humor reaches its apex with what may be the most astounding of the practical jokes. Whenever there is an audience seated for a concert or a poetry reading, and presumably the people are enraptured by the music or the verse, presto!, a large number of jets of water begin their caper. The spouting stuff soars all over

and seems to be falling from the sky, thus holding in captivity and captivating every person in his seat. But no one ever gets drenched.

The aquatic pranks at the Villa Lante are, in point of fact, only a small part of the real magic of this fascinating, thoroughly neglected tourist treasure. Each of the sixteen main fountains (with such names as Fountain of the Octagon, Fountain of the Lion Cubs, Fountain of the Little Madonna, Fountain of the Beaver, etc.) is worth your special attention, because most of them emanate from the mouths of enormous stone masks, skip from terrace to terrace or dance over rocks and statues of gods. One of the fountains actually runs through a central groove in a huge stone table which was once used to keep food cool. The water from these various fountains eventually makes its way to four sleepy little lakes entwined graciously around the Fountain of the Moors in the center of a huge flowerbed, but not before most of the water trickles and gurgles down the center of a flight of steps in a chain of interlocking basins.

Begun at the end of the fifteenth century by a powerful Catholic family and owned for centuries by cardinals (during which time several Popes visited), the Villa came into the hands of the Lante family as a gift from Pope Alexander VII in the 1600's. The fountains and tricks were constructed by Tommaso Chinucci, a hydraulic engineer who wanted to create a symphony of charming *aqua pura* in many movements with a *coda* of *allegro* surprises. Thanks to him, "The Villa of the Sixteen Fountains" not only drips the light fantastic but also makes, methinks, quite a splash.

A MUSEUM FORTY-FIVE MILLION YEARS OLD

THERE ARE NO ifs and buts about which is the world's oldest museum. Give or take a few months, it is about forty-five million years old and was put together by a non-scientist who has the strangest job—he hunts fossils for a living.

About thirty miles northeast of Verona, tourists in Bolca will find a rustic museum that beats anything yet. Situated nearly three thousand feet above sea level, amid cherry orchards and chestnut woods, are the home and museum of Massimiliano Cerato, whose tag-line could well be: "Have hammer, will travel."

Cerato's hammer has been busy since he was a seven-year-old boy—like the hammers of his father, grandfather and great-grandfather before him, who for over two hundred years chopped fossils out of what is perhaps the richest concentrated fossil field in the world. The some fifty caves in which these specimens are to be found are on land owned by the Cerato family.

What gives Cerato's museum a stupendous scientific and tourist appeal is that more than two hundred of the species of fish and the hundred-odd species of crustaceans and mollusks he has dug out of his caves have disappeared from earth. Moreover, Cerato has uncovered about eighty marine plants which also no longer grow anywhere on this planet.

Cerato's biological curios are nearly all in a perfect state of preservation, even down to the original colors of the animals and plants when they were alive during the middle of the Tertiary Period (Eocene) forty-five to fifty million years ago. You can visit the Cerato family's private museum (admission: sixteen cents), which is in a modern structure attached to his one-family home atop Bolca's highest hill, any morning between 10:00 and 12:00 or any afternoon between 2:30 and 6:00, except on Mondays.

Though Cerato's museum has only been open since 1969, he can boast of some quite distinguished visitors, such as the King of Sweden. And, many years ago, the Cerato family was honored by a personal visit from Emperor Franz Joseph of Austria who begged permission to extend his stay because he was fascinated by the petrified life from the womb of the earth. The fossil given to the Emperor then is now on proud display in a Vienna museum.

In some forty years of work, Massimiliano Cerato has extracted over 100,000 fossils, of which perhaps about two thousand are of interest to the average layman. He dug out his greatest discovery about twenty-five years ago—a magnificent blue prehistoric crocodile almost six feet long. Another major find was the only known example of an extinct fish called *platax plinianus* which, with its delicate feathery fins, can be seen in all its original colors in a stratum of green rock that makes it look as if it is still swimming.

Working today in the petrified lagoon of Bolca, fossil-hunter Cerato uses a sixth sense as he hammer-taps a wall in one of his caves. Once he decides to cut, he isolates the section of slab by digging around it so that it sticks out. Then, with a few master strokes, he separates the stone slab from the wall. The slabs are opened like an oyster by hitting them on the top with sharp light blows, using the wedge end of the hammer. If the slab divides properly, one side will contain the animal or plant in relief on the stone and the other side will have the concave counterpart.

Massimiliano Cerato, at age 48, holds another distinction. Without even a high school education, he is one of the world's few self-taught scientists, having become a respected paleontologist. Both Professor Jacques Blot, a paleontologist from France, and Professor Lorenzo Sorbini, a geologist for the Italian government, claim that, in the three years they dug with Cerato, they learned something new every day from him.

Modest about his knowledge, Cerato merely explains it away by saying:

"We Ceratos have fossils in our blood. It is like a sickness. For me, when I go to work, it is like going fishing—but the fish I catch are not so fresh."

It is true Cerato's fish are a bit old, but what man today could tell as many fish stories with so much dig-nity?

Fossil hunter Massimiliano Cerato and some of his fossil specimens.

ITALY'S FOUR-LEGGED HITCHHIKER

ITALY IS A BOOT that from the toe up shows every tourist it has a jumbo jumble of attractions. But, while roaming the kneecap part of Italy in search of sculpture by Michelangelo, Donatello, Bernini *et al.*, do not forget to look in on Lampo the Traveling Dog, in its own way one of the most arresting statues in all Italy.

Here at the main train station of Campiglia Marittima, within sight of Elba island, stands a gleaming memorial to a mongrel called Lampo, beloved by every trainman in Italy. There is a tale wagging behind that statue, a happy story with a sad ending, but perhaps Lampo's little story is no story at all.

The monument here to the Traveling Dog compels you to look at it. It shows Lampo seated on a pedestal of stone, holding his right paw aloft. Facing the railroad tracks, he watches the trains as they come in and go out.

Born in the United States and taken to Italy in 1953 while still a puppy by American sailors, Lampo—like Rin Tin Tin and Lassie—was no stranger to Italian television. And just about every newspaper in the country managed to do a big feature about the little dog who had the most unusual hobby any dog ever had.

The inscription around the base of the statue does not tell anything about the bowwow celebrity. But the personnel working at the train station can explain. Better still, seek out Lampo's owner, Elvio Barlettani, the assistant station master who wrote and published a book about the mongrel, and you will get all the details.

"What Lampo did," explains the 47-year-old railway man who adopted the white dog, "was to live a life different from that of other dogs. Lampo liked traveling in trains—and because he got to know their schedules and could distinguish the slow trains from the expresses, he managed to go somewhere every day by train. But he always made sure he would not go beyond a certain spot on the map, so as to catch the proper connection which would take him back to Campiglia Marittima before dawn."

Lampo, whose name in Italian means "flash of lightning," made over 3,000 trips in his day. When he took his first long journey, all the way to Rome, Barlettani got a call from the station master there, asking whether they should put the dog on the proper train for home. Barlettani said no, let the dog find his own way back. Sure enough, late that evening, Lampo jumped off the Rome-Turin express at the Campiglia Marittima station.

After that there was no stopping the Traveling Dog. His fame spread. Platform workers everywhere would affectionately tie all kinds of railway ticket stubs to his collar to indicate where he had been. Some of the staff even stuck imitation tickets on his tail with the words, "Free Pass For Lampo," and anybody who tried to take away these special passes would get a ferocious snarl from the railroad rover.

"We came to learn," adds Barlettani, "that Lampo visited every station in northwest Italy at least once. He was a very sociable dog, and he knew which cars to board on any train where some-

Statue of Lampo, the traveling dog, at Campiglia Marittima station.

one on duty or a tourist might give him a bite to eat. Since he had the job of escorting my daughter Mirna to school every morning, he made only short trips on schooldays and saved his longer journeys for weekends."

Only once in eight years did Lampo miss a return train. That was the time he went past his stop. Eventually he got back to his home station by taking a series of connecting trains and back-tracking—a feat, say the local railway men, that could only have been done by a person who had a printed timetable in his hands.

Lampo's railroad career came to an end on the evening of July 22, 1961. Ironically, the four-legged hitchhiker died under the wheels of a freight train, the kind he had always avoided because passenger trains were his preference.

The accident happened at the Campiglia Marittima station, following an illness which had kept him indoors. He was not at his canine best that day and even needed a boost from a trainman to help him scramble up the steps of a local.

Today Lampo has come back to the Campiglia Marittima station to stand guard over the train traffic. There are some people who swear that the lifelike statue lets out a bark of approval whenever a train pulls in exactly on schedule. They claim Lampo wants his beloved trains to do everything in a correct way and to put on the dog.

Pharmacist Marta Stefani Bernardini.

THE RIGHT PRESCRIPTION FOR TOURISM

THE OLDEST practicing pharmacy in the world gives every tourist in Florence a dose of his own medicine, the right prescription for any traveler who needs a site for sore eyes.

A hop, skip and a jump from Florence's main railroad station is the Officina Profumo Farmaceutica di Santa Maria Novella di Firenze (situated at Via della Scala 16), a drug store without par anywhere in the universe. Opened in 1612 by monks, the Florence pharmacy draws tourist buses as often as it does ordinary customers.

Where else can a customer sit in a Savonarola chair and admire frescoes by Giotto and Spinello Aretino, among a collection of Renaissance faience vases and jars, while waiting for his prescription to be filled? Where else can he be served by a proprietress who seems to have stepped out of the Renaissance, wearing a white coat purchased from the UPIM department store around the corner?

"All of our products are originals," explains Madame Marta Stefani Bernardini, whose family has owned the pharmacy for nearly a century. "We do not sell products distributed by companies. Our medicines, perfumes, liqueurs and cosmetics are concocted according to formulas worked out by monks in the seventeenth century. Yet we do not want for clients. Our liqueurs, for instance, are ordered by the Vatican, and they include sweet elixir of rhubarb and sweet elixir of cinchona. Many movie stars, quite a few from Hollywood, come here to get our rice powder. In the past we used to supply the Queen of England and the Queen of Romania quite regularly with iris flower soap and sachet."

Madame Stefani Bernardini reluctantly talks about the possibility of a famous ghost haunting the premises. According to a prevailing theory, the ghost filtered into the pharmacy at the time of the Napoleonic invasion when a rich treasure was allegedly hidden there. No one has ever seen this so-called spirit nor ever located the treasure. Yet many nights of the year "queer sounds" are reverberating among the Doric columns.

Some of the very big sellers at the Santa Maria Novella pharmacy include the perfumes which are always called "essences—because they are not perfumes." Among those sold are triple and quadruple essences for handkerchiefs, also essences that evaporate quickly—some of which are used by customers to pep up desserts.

Another item of note is the world's oldest medicine, Teriaca, which began with Mithridates who died sixty-three years before Christ. The formula passed into the hands of Nero's doctor, who added a few things of his own and launched it upon an amazing career. Original Teriaca was made from balsam fruit, myrrh, nard, Cretan dittany, Celtic spikenard, Jewish bitumen, earth from Lemnos and balm of Gilead. Today Teriaca is made of nutmeg butter, hyssop, *imperico*, clarified butter, gentian root, *comedrios* and *ivatetica*. Any questions?

During the Middle Ages Teriaca was taken for everything from bubonic plague to ingrown toenails. The Florence pharmacy makes up a supply every thirty years (there is not much call for it anymore), but if you venture to buy some at sixteen dollars a smidgin and taste it, it will remind you of quinine. Remember to ask for a portion that is not mixed with earthworm.

Somewhat cheaper in price is the pharmacy's popular anti-hysterical waters selling for about fifty cents a tiny bottle. There is also an aromatic vinegar sold in a purse-sized souvenir flacon which has the Santa Maria Novella emblem embossed on it and reads: "For Sniffing Only." And for $1.60 you can pick up a concoction called potpourri which will perfume closets and drawers.

If you ask Mrs. Stefani Bernardini to give you a take-home copy of the pharmacy's picturesque price list (rolled up with red ribbon), the chances are she will and also take you on a tour of some of the eye-arresting salons in the back. As do the vestibule and the main sales room, the inside quarters resemble an art museum.

This fascinating relic of the pharmaceutical past applies a secret formula to intoxicate everyone who enters its portals because it has the right dope.

A LIVING CHESS GAME

EVEN IF YOU DO NOT play chess, you won't be caught with your pawns down when you visit Marostica on the day of the legendary chess game played on a checkerboard big enough for tennis. No matter who comes out on top, white king or black king, the tourist is definitely the winner here.

Every other September during even-numbered years the city of Marostica re-enacts a 500-year-old chess contest in front of the fourteenth-century Basso Castle, incorporating some impressive medieval pomp. Actors wearing the curious costumes of the period make the various moves across the gigantic chessboard, the world's largest, as a herald calls out each move with stentorian authority.

It's indeed a spectacle as hundreds of kibitzers and tourists stand or sit along the sides and cheer for black rook or white bishop. Marostica revived this jumbo chess game to woo tourists away from nearby Venice and apparently the city has succeeded.

Spectacular beyond description, the game is based on one played in the year 1454—but therein lies a true, heartwarming love story of nobility and chivalry that needs telling from the beginning. So. . . .

Once upon a time there was a good, good, governor of Marostica. His name was Taddeo Parisio and he opposed any form of bloodshed. The governor had a beautiful daughter whose name was Lionora, with whom a pair of young noblemen—handsome and gallant knights, both of them—fell in love.

The two courting courtiers, Vieri da Vallorana and Rinaldo d'Angarano,

both wanted to marry Lionora and were indeed on the verge of settling the issue with a duel to the death. But the father, the good governor of Marostica, said no. There was to be no blood spilled for the hand of his daughter. He issued the following decree:

"Upon pain of beheading, said single and bloody combat be not made in any case whatsoever. But the challenge, which will have as its prize the marriage of the winner with my daughter Lionora, shall take the form of a combat at the noble game of chess with big, living pieces all armed and distinguished with their noble colors."

As a consolation prize, the loser had the option of marrying Lionora's younger sister, Oldrada. So that all the townspeople could follow the moves better, Governor Parisio had the plays repeated by live chessmen moving on the marble squares that were affixed onto the piazza in front of the castle.

Vieri da Vallorana emerged the victor that day and there followed a grandiose celebration in Marostica for the double wedding. Today that odd chess game is commemorated in Marostica every second year. Because the moves of the original game are now forgotten, the players enact Schlechter's classic game of 1891 in which checkmate is effected in forty moves.

To put it mildly, Marostica's day of drama is quite a show, as trumpets blare and the town crier reads the official challenge to the players. With the castle bedecked in the flying colors of both knights, actors in their fifteenth-century regalia play out the parts of Governor Parisio, Lionora, the knights Vallorana

and Angarano and all the others. After a mighty fanfare announces the end of the chess game, the colorful proceedings continue, with soldiers singing the battle song of Marostica. A cannon boom ends the festa but not before the full array of the knights in armor comes to attention before Governor Parisio and salutes him by shouting "Lion!" three times, the ancient Marostican equivalent of "For he's a jolly good fellow!"

Biannual chess game at Marostica is played in front of the old castle with actors in costumes as the chess pieces (PHOTO BY EZIO ANDRETTA).

History tells us that Lionora was very beautiful, that she turned out to be a marvelous wife, that she bore her husband fine children and that in marrying the lucky knight she could not have made a better move.

101

A SEVEN-RING CIRCUS CLOCK

TRAVELERS WHO ENTER this panoramic door of Sicily, a handshake away from the Italian mainland, are invariably startled and a bit amused to see street vendors selling ice cream on a soft hamburger bun. Another thing one remembers about Messina is its Barnumesque clock.

A clock like this is the wonder of touristdom. No other place in Italy boasts a timepiece like the one housed in the belltower of Messina's twelfth-

Messina clock tower.

century basilica. Over two hundred feet high, the big ticker is a mechanical-historical-ecclesiastical-astronomical nonesuch, a something-to-write-home-about rarity.

In each of seven levels, or stories, the chronometrical marvel has gold-encrusted statues that swing into motion at certain times of the day. Starting with the bottom "scene," there are movable figurines that show the four ages of man—infancy, adolescence, maturity and old age.

When it is fifteen minutes after the hour, the clock rings and the figure of a baby passes across the statue in front of a human skeleton that waves its staff menacingly. On the half hour, the statue of a boy walks in front of the threatening skeleton which represents Death. Then, as the three-quarter hour is reached, a soldier marches through. Precisely at the hour, comes the turn of a decrepit old man.

Meanwhile, up on another story there is a pair of large gilded statues of Messina's two war heroines, Dina and Chiarenza, who tug the ropes that strike the bells. It is a good show any hour of the day, but your best bet is to come for a look-see at noontime. That is when all the tourist guides bring their flocks for the fabulous twelve o'clock performance, when the whole contraption stirs into full action like a seven-ring circus. It goes like this:

As the four ages of man pass in review in front of Death and the two heroines are banging the large bells, up on top, a yellow lion with a jeweled crown rises on his hind legs, turns three times while wagging his tail, veers his head towards the piazza and emits three stentorian M.G.M. roars.

Almost simultaneously, a large rooster spreads out his wings and lets forth a triple cockledoodledoo that can be heard all over town. Suddenly, a dove emerges moments before a miniature church rolls out on stage. A level higher, one of four solemn religious scenes (depending on the time of the year) comes up for display.

During all this, a flying angel announces the arrival of the Virgin Mary, who is followed by the Apostle Paul and four of Messina's historical heroes. Mary stops while some of the figurines pass by her. Now an angel delivers a letter which Mary blesses, and then the letter is picked up by Paul who takes it with him.

The whole thing takes a full ten minutes. But that's not all. . . .

The clock also runs a weekly calendar. The pieces function almost imperceptibly so that it takes twenty-four hours for, say Wednesday (represented by Mercury), to change into Thursday (Jupiter). Coupled with this is the perpetual calendar which indicates the date, month, year and season.

Perhaps the most remarkable part of the clock is its astronomical calendar. Showing each of the nine planets, it is rigged to accomplish the rotations according to the actual precise speed of the planets. For instance, the disc representing Mars takes exactly 686 days, 22 hours, 18 minutes and 43 seconds to complete a full turn—exactly what the planet takes to go once around the sun.

Given as a gift by the friar engineers of Strasbourg in 1933 (to commemorate Messina's destruction by the 1908 earthquake), the big clock loses no time in impressing all spectators. The only time it does lose, however, is with its minute hand in one of the belltower's faces that runs a bit slow.

But then, Messina's horological opera, giving a glad hand to all tourists, does not have a face that would stop a clock.

Villa Palagonia.

LET TOURISTS COME together and they invariably get around to talking about horrible places they have been to. The most "horrible" place in all Europe, however, may be at Bagheria on the north coast of Sicily, some twenty-five miles east of Palermo. If you can imagine a place deliberately designed to keep people away—nay, to scare them off!—then indeed pay a call on the Villa Palagonia, a dilapidated building surrounded by an array of horrendous gargoyles, horrifying serpents, horrid dragons and horrific human figures. Suffice to say you will be horror-stricken by the sight of these horrible monsters.

Ah, but wait! Steady now! There's more. Behind this most horrible of horror collections is a sorrowful tale of love and devotion. It is the true and touching story of the ugliest man who ever lived.

They still talk about him in Sicily. They say that God put on the face of the Prince of Palagonia, Ferdinando Francesco Gravina, every blemish and defect conceivable, making him utterly repulsive. His oversized lips met crookedly under a hook-like nose set at an oblique angle. Beneath a pair of savage, ill-matched brows, he squinted through piercing half-closed eyelids. His bloodshot eyeballs and his misshapen bald pate gave him a look of ferocity that blended grotesquely into a keg-sized torso with tiny shoulders.

Living a life of torment, the freakish prince kept to himself in melancholy isolation in his dark, dreary palace. Despite his noble birth and the wealth of his family, folks in town shunned him like the plague. Yet they felt genuinely sorry for him.

Then the impossible happened. Nobody believed it when the news came. All Sicily was abuzz. Bagheria's ugly duck had miraculously managed to woo and win the hand of the belle of Sicilian nobility, the lovely Maria Gioacchina Gaetani, daughter of a rich duke.

It did not take long for the beauteous Maria to make Villa Palagonia resound with festive gatherings. For the first time, music and laughter were heard

104

A MONUMENT TO MELANCHOLY

where, in the past, emptiness had echoed. Ferdinando, now proud, carried himself like a nobleman, and people ceased whispering about his hideous face while marveling that the most desirable woman in all the Mediterranean had fallen in love with a man so forbiddingly homely.

Alas, soon a crisis came to the strange union. The prince discovered that his adored wife was keeping nocturnal trysts with other men. Ferdinando did not know what to do. He spent his days praying that Maria would respond to the honest love he had for her. But it did not work.

Grief-stricken beyond endurance, the ugly man began to lose his power of reason. He became obsessed with a fantastic scheme to imprison Maria behind the palace walls. Knowing how easily his wife became frightened, he decided to surround his villa with statues so terrifying that they would likely deter her from roaming off at night. Moreover, the distraught prince believed he would exact a perverse revenge by making some of the macabre figures in the image of Maria's lovers.

The prince commissioned an artist named Tommaso di Napoli to make the strange architectural sculptures. In all, some two hundred images were put up, half of them lining the path to the gate, while the other half straddled the walls around the building.

And, wonder of wonders, the strange plan actually succeeded. For, after the unveiling of the statuary, Maria stayed inside. In tomb-like peace, the couple lived there until 1788, when the Prince died at the age of sixty-five. His wife passed on a few years later.

Prince Ferdinando's unbeautiful monuments can be visited from nine in the morning till sundown seven days a week. It won't be long before time and the ravages of weather take their final, inevitable toll of one of Italy's most unusual tourist attractions—overlooked for the most part by the tourist tide that washes over Sicily every summer—for the statues and the Villa Palagonia are slowly crumbling away. To everyone's horror. . . .

105

THE PIED PIPER OF HAMELIN

SEVEN HUNDRED YEARS later, whether a fairy tale or not, the truth of the matter is that the Pied Piper of Hamelin is very much alive in this gingerbread-and-cobblestone town on the banks of the Weser River where the captivating houses are half stone and half timber with their painted decorations and devout mottoes inscribed on the outside.

You must come to Hamelin at least once in your life. As everybody knows, this is the town that a mysterious stranger and his magic flute made eternally world famous when he led first the rats and then the kiddies away, never again to return. Though ordinarily a visitor might expect a certain amount of commercial exploitation here, the city fathers have said Nein! Nein! to any take-the-tourist-trickery. So there is mighty little of it.

True, you can buy hard little breads in the form of a rat (including a set of brittle whiskers), and you can even buy a phonograph record in English which gives you snatches of the Pied Piper's theme song and narrates his historic yarn. Those who want to pursue the legend even further can visit Das Rattenfängerhaus ("the rat catcher's house") which, built in 1603, has now become the town's finest and most picturesque restaurant.

But perhaps most engaging of all Hamelin's attractions is the genial reenactment of the en masse abduction of the town's small fry on that fateful June 26th in the year 1284. Every Sunday afternoon, at about one o'clock (come early if you want a good place to stand) between May and the end of September, you can watch a two-act play of the world's most famous kidnaping, done by seventy-five well-rehearsed tiny tot actors and the local postman, who plays the vengeful Pied Piper.

Invariably, as you watch the show in the square in front of the town hall, you cannot help wondering if the Pied Piper really did exist. Did this musical mystery man actually blow his hocus-pocus tooter and decoy the pestilent rats of Hamelin into the river and later hex all the kids into a mountain? Well, Hamelin's authorities and local experts firmly insist that the ancient whodunit, which sounds like Agatha Christie *mit Sauerbraten*, is no folktale.

Working independently of each other, several German scholars have inspected thousands of yellowed documents and manuscripts and have come up with like answers. Apparently the story is quite true. But! Here are the facts:

One dogged investigator, after years of meticulous Teutonic detective work, uncovered a crumbly manuscript handwritten in Latin by a monk in the year 1370 which stated: "In Hamelin in the year 1284, there occurred a wondrous event on the feast of St. John and St. Paul. A young man of about 30 years, handsome and well-clothed so that all who saw him admired him, entered Hamelin by the Weser Gate. He began piping through town on a silver flute. And all the children, to the number of 130, followed him out the East Gate. There by Calvary Cross they suddenly vanished. . . ."

Although this account made no mention of the rodents, from other manuscripts it was learned that the rat-drowning theme was tacked on centuries later by imaginative writers. Still another scholar hunted down evidence that fits into the above version like the parts of a jigsaw puzzle.

In the year 1285, a German military bishop who lived ten miles down the river from Hamelin began a recruiting drive for people to serve in towns he had founded. The bishop sent out labor agents to convince groups of youths to emigrate from overcrowded Hamelin for a chance at a better life elsewhere. In effect, then—so far as the legend is concerned—the bishop's recruiters were made into the image of the Pied Piper and the wanderlusty volunteers were transformed into the children.

This version seems to have gained a solid acceptance.

Finally . . . er, what about the one thousand guilders the Pied Piper was supposed to have received from Hamelin for giving the boot to Mickey Rodent? At the usual interest rates, the accumulated unpaid debt would today run into millions of dollars. *Ach, Du lieber Gott,* maybe that's why there is no one who will pay the piper.

Hamelin's
Sunday morning reenactment
of the Pied Piper story.

A NONSENSE MUSEUM

A toothpick with fur, for winter use.

A TOOTHPICK WITH FUR, for winter use.

A poisoned bullet, the size of a basketball.

A sample of Berlin air in a bottle, a glass nail, a container of cold steam and a burning wax candle (with electric plug)—these bits of nonsense and others await the unsuspecting tourist in the Bavarian capital who wanders into what may be the goofiest museum on the face of the earth.

Housed in the south tower of Munich's fourteenth-century Isar Gate is the Karl Valentin Museum, perhaps the world's only public array of tomfoolery. Though hardly known to outsiders, the "Nonsense Museum" has been tickling the marrow of Munich residents and German tourists since it first opened almost twenty years ago.

The queer collection primarily represents examples of Herr Karl Valentin's "profoundly philosophical sense of humor, which was a testimony to his wisdom," so sayeth one German scholar. Valentin, before his untimely death in 1948, was a well-known traveling music hall comedian, a laughing philosopher revered and adored by Germans during his heyday, the twenties and thirties. Affectionately known as "K.V.," Karl Valentin spent a lifetime (with his sidekick, Liesl Karlstadt) demonstrating through his unique brand of humor "how ridiculous and unimportant man becomes when fate starts throwing tiny pebbles into the works." Many Germans who visit the Karl Valentin Museum and guffaw their way through do not consider the "Nonsense Museum" nonsense at all.

A visitor entering the museum wends his way upward along an enclosed spiral staircase to the first of three landings. On the way up he is confronted on both sides of the stair walls with funnybone exhibits, some of which are not readily understandable to a foreign tourist unless he is aptly armed with a dictionary. One of the first exhibits on the stairway is a jacket "worn by a porter of Westend Street when he had the bad luck to first meet his wife." Still further up is a partially melted piece of sculpture made of wax "which had the misfortune of being near the radiator." On the first landing you are immediately confronted with the Karl Valentin solution to the parking problem—a baby carriage. Overhead hangs a ghost drum for a midnight closing signal to the museum's public. But the drum is never used since the museum shuts its doors at six p.m.

The "Nonsense Museum" also features a plain brick, described as the tuffet that Little Miss Muffet sat on (petrified), the apple that Adam bit, a chamber pot with chain and handle for flushing, a rope to hang yourself with (which for lack of funds has only been painted on the wall), a genuine cockroach of the Munich kitchen variety (loaned by a private zoo) and a beautifully framed solid black portrait, showing a chimney sweep at night. Displayed in addition is a model of the Vesuvius volcano with a "No Smoking" sign attached. Nearby, there is a doll with a huge mustache, representing a man who has been over-rejuvenated by doctors. Next to this is a pan full of water. According to the caption, this is "liquid snow sculpture, a thing of rare beauty when still in its solid state."

The Museum also has dried sunbeams locked up in a safe, a riding harness that is out of order, a piece of glue (hardened), spectacles for people who are hard of hearing and a picture of the only man who ever filled out his income tax form properly (he died very young of premature exhaustion of the brain).

K.V.'s curious collection of calculated comedy, however, overlooks one deft touch that could be considered his "masterpiece of ironic humor." The German laugh merchant had the last laugh on the world when he passed away in 1948. As might have been expected, and to the surprise of no one, he died on All Fools' Day.

HEIDELBERG'S STUDENT PRISON

TOURISTS WHO COME TO THIS proud old town, famous for its university and "The Student Prince," invariably are attracted to a sight not listed in the guide book. This is the Heidelberg University student prison, where rowdy campus offenders used to be sent for terms ranging from one to five weeks on a diet of bread and water—which sometimes ended up being pretzels and beer (the German version of the former).

Until 1914, the centuries-old school administered intramural justice by sentencing prank-happy students to its own clink for a cooling-off period. Although many students were not fond of the jug, there were others who found in it "a great place to get away from it all."

Some of the inmates of the *Studentenkarzer* later were to become famous in their own right. According to the University's records, one of them became ambassador to the United States and another became ambassador to the Court of St. James in England. Even Bismarck's son, Herbert, knew the inside of the prison. In fact, he served five sentences there altogether—one of them for putting a chamber pot on the head of a statue near the administration building.

The most common "crime" in those days was the pilfering of stones from buildings and throwing them through police windows with a note that said: "We found this in the street." The penalty for this folly was the maximum— thirty-five days on bread and water with no parole.

In actuality the bread and water punishment rarely encompassed difficulties, for the students learned quickly that there was more than one

way to unlatch the hatch. Fellow students and the girl friend of the "convict" would sneak around to the bad-boy bastille with picnic boxes of food and beer and quietly haul them up by rope (the beer first) to the top-floor chamber. Sometimes the girl herself would shin up to the barred window and give her locked-up lover a few kisses for dessert.

The Heidelberg University calaboose was located on the last landing of an apartment house at Number 2 Austiner-Strasse. It had four cells, each of which carried a nickname—Palais Royal, Sans-souci, Solitude and Grand Hotel. The cells provided only an iron bed frame (no mattress) and a splintery table. Following his conviction by University officials, a student had to undergo a prescribed ritual before the cell door was clanked shut. Humiliated, he was taken to the coop in a procession, riding backwards on a donkey and carrying his own mattress.

About a hundred years ago, one undergraduate started the practice of leaving a message on his cell wall. With paint that had been smuggled in and the wax from a melting candle, plus soot, white bread and saliva, he drew his silhouette on the wall. After that, nearly every student left behind a written or sketched reminder for posterity that he had served time there.

Today tourists who visit the one-time prison (visitors have included Mark Twain and Mamie Eisenhower) can peruse the schoolboy decorations and such references as "One for all and all for one" dramatically hand-printed over the walls. Facial silhouettes in profile seem to have been the preferred

act of the inmates. One such silhouette belonged to an American sophomore from San Francisco (foreign students were not immune to serving a rap) whose name was Max Salomon. On March 14, 1889, in the cell called Solitude, he left a terse declaration of his views on Heidelberg University and its

Section of wall of Heidelberg University prison.

prison. In large capital letters in red, white and blue, outlined with a fancy red border, he wrote a one-word editorial expressing his opinion: RATS.

111

DACHSHUND VILLAGE

SOUVENIR-HUNTING TOURISTS who are looking for "something really different" in the way of a travel memento could come here to this tiny Bavarian hamlet about thirty miles northwest of Passau on the Austrian border and pick up a living souvenir—*the* souvenir to end all souvenirs.

Gergweis is not to be found on many maps of Germany, but in the dog-lovers' world, this town of five hundred people is the center of the universe—because there are more dachshunds living here (750 by last official census count) than people. Small wonder, therefore, that Gergweis is better known by its nickname, *Dackeldorf* ("Dachshund Village").

Nearly every resident here is engaged in the business of raising and selling puppy frankfurter dogs—with customers in every country on earth. It is dogmatically claimed that just about every dachshund in the world can trace an ancestor or even his own birth to Gergweis, which has shipped out (by special delivery air mail) a half million pups.

The queen of the breeders, nay the champ, is "Dachshund Katie," a graying, plumpish grandma who for over forty years has been the town's unofficial mayor, publicist and genial greeter of all tourists who come for a look-see, even if they do not pick up a live souvenir to take home. Dachshund Katie—or Frau Kathie Dorfmeister—brims over with friendliness and super-personality as she chatters about her favorite subject while taking you around her well-equipped compound of elongated low-to-the-ground canines. She raises about 150 at a time,

but the barking of her progeny can often sound like a chorus of 1,500.

One of Frau Dorfmeister's specialties is the hunting dachshund. Picking out the likely candidates for intensive training among her two-year-olds, she puts them through a thorough daily instruction session during which she weeds out the ones who just don't have it. Trained mostly to accompany duck hunters, Katie's tailwaggers—when they get their diplomas, complete with ribbon, red seal and melted wax—are capable of swimming several miles to pick up a felled duck and bring it back.

"Many people don't know," Katie relates, "that the dachshund was first bred artificially about eighty years ago as a cross between the hunting terrier and the spaniel to make a special kind of hunting dog out of him, one small enough to get down into narrow burrows, having a bark loud enough to scare a badger out of the other end and into the open. Today the hunting dachshund is not used for chasing after badgers, but he is an awfully intelligent dog whose quick mind lends itself to all kinds of hunting problems that few other dogs are able to cope with."

Katie's adoration for the dachshund is also manifest by the way she cares for them. In addition to a gleaming kitchen where gourmet doggie-bags are prepared for the bowwow bunch, she even has an "Old Dogs' Home" on her grounds in which her oldest pals, some of them twenty years of age, are kept in splendiferous retirement. At great expense, she refuses to have any of her senior citizen studs put away, after they no longer have an appetite for fathering pups. Like everyone else in Dachshund Village, Katie sells her dogs for rates that range from $60 to $125 (plus postage), the final price being determined by the length of the dog's hair. Long-haired dogs sell more cheaply, whereas dogs with short hair who are qualified graduate hunters fall into the top-price category.

How did a Bavarian housewife become the world's top dachshund breeder?

A dog lover supreme before her marriage, Katie owned thirty stray dogs of all species and, to pay for their upkeep, she decided to make some money breeding the quadrupeds. Because the dachshund was the most prolific, she concentrated on him and, within a few years, other people in Gergweis followed suit. In time the whole town went dachshund, and today Gergweis has become the dachshund capital of the world, complete with a dachshund hospital, dachshund veterinarians, dachshund schools, dachshund maternity centers, a dachshund newspaper, a dachshund library and a dachshund information bureau for anybody who wants to write in.

Yes, Gergweis—thanks to Dachshund Katie—is one town that has really gone to the dogs.

"Dachshund Katie"
with some of her neighbors
in Dachshund Village.

Finger-wrestling.

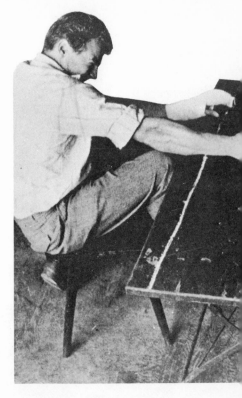

GERMANY'S DIGIT-YANKING SPORT

THERE ARE SOME hale Germans in this Bavarian hamlet of Ruhpolding who brag they have more strength in one finger of their right hand than the world's heavyweight boxing champ has in his whole right arm.

At first, this sounds like just another idle boast until you find out that the man is an expert at *Fingerhäkeln* (finger-wrestling), a cozy sort of sport that goes back to the fourteenth century and never ceases to stun tourists who come here when the digit-yanking season is under way in the early fall.

The rules of *Fingerhäkeln* are simple. Two men (occasionally a woman engages in the game) sit across from each other at a table with white lines chalked lengthwise down the center.

Each man puts his middle finger into the same leather loop, and at the word "*Auf!*" begins with ferocity and accompanying grunts to tug away from his opponent.

A hefty finger-wrestler, if he gets the jump on his adversary, can often pull him across the table in ignominious belly-whop style with one deft jerk of his talented talon. It does not matter what kind of work a fellow does for a living—it's all in the finger muscle. That is why a big, strapping mountain man may go down in defeat wrestling a cook.

The men in Bavaria who have become pretty good at yanking one another's joints spend many hours building up their finger muscle by pull-

114

locale in town—take your pick. The contestants dress in leather knickers and green felt hats, a kind of unofficial uniform for the highly regarded matches. Sitting across from each other at oak tables, with their legs wrapped around steel stools, they engage in their tug-of-war often with noses bleeding because of the strain.

In the finals it is not unusual for both Goliaths to approach the last bout with bandaged fingers, casualties of previous wars. Although both men are usually in pain, they stagger to the arena after fortifying themselves with several steins of beer, as many as a dozen in some cases, while the big brass band, oompahing the "Finger-Wrestling Hymn," helps create the proper fighting spirit.

Though the Bavarian fad is over six hundred years old, nobody really knows how *Fingerhäkeln* got started. It is believed to have sprung up in German saloons where a man in search of free beer could win many a stein-full if he had perfected his tug-testing techniques. Also, the game is believed to have been played to impress females and win their favor. Since women are the best-liked items in Germany, next to beer, you can see how by combining both, finger-wrestling became a popular indoor sport. Hence it did not take long for the local *Brauer* to get into the act. Seeing a way to spark the sale of more beer, and in some instances enough to flood the Brenner Pass, the neighborhood brewery sponsored regional finger-grappling contests. These local matches eventually led to the national event held every year in or near Munich. Anybody can come and watch—or participate.

ing at whatever happens to be handy. A favorite practice gimmick is to drag a wagon full of hay up a hill by one finger. Some contestants make arrangements to pull a railroad freight car (unloaded), while others will spend hours leaning over a well with a bucket of water suspended from their middle finger. The preferred exercise of 51-year-old Willi Lehner, a heavyweight stonemason who is one of the proclaimed champs of all time, is to hang suspended by his middle finger from a hook screwed into an overhead beam and raise himself a few inches at a time.

Apart from the annual September/October "World Series," there are nightly competitions here in Ruhpolding in practically every beer-drinking

To become a success at *Fingerhäkeln*, you need a lot of pull.

COLLECTED CURIOSA, GERMAN STYLE

WHATEVER IT IS IN A national character that makes people collect things, this trait certainly comes out strong in Germany's multiplicity of oddball museums. If you have a fervor for miscellanea which agitates your curiosity barometer, then you should give high priority to some of this country's museums devoted to the daffier aspects of teutonic collectomania. The assembled curiosa run a range all the way from soup to wallpaper, from bedbugs to torture instruments, from bread to dollhouses.

Dollhouses? Well, if these are your cup of tea, then try Nuremberg. One of the most interesting of all museums—especially for women and children—is the German National Museum at Nuremberg which features the best group of dollhouses anywhere. Some of the houses are over three hundred years old, stand six feet high and are completely furnished down to the most minute detail. Viewers who come for a quick look usually end up spending hours inspecting the superb craftsmanship and marveling at the patience that went into making the intricate furnishings. One dollhouse might be outstanding for its tiny folded linens peeking from a partially opened bureau, while another will excite all visitors because it has running water coming from the wee faucets or because the dining room table is laid, complete with individual silverware and little-bitsy candles.

Now, should dolls not excite, an attraction that certainly will is the bedbug museum of the medieval Bavarian city of Aschaffenburg, a few miles southeast of Frankfurt. Housed on the fourth floor of a rickety local schoolhouse, the collection offers 403 different varieties. The bugs on display in glass cases are not alive, of course, and they represent the accumulation of the late Dr. Karl Singer, a city health official who had many of the insects shipped to him from all over the globe.

Museum buffs would also do well to look into the Cuckoo Clock Museum at

Dollhouse in Nuremberg.

Triberg in the Black Forest. Here the call of the little wooden bird—whose song is indeed heard all over the world—comes from clocks that display some ingenious details and charming gimmickry. Since all the timepieces are kept in good running order, it is better for the eardrums that you leave before the hour strikes twelve, when begins a birdsong chorus that will really drive you cuckoo.

The only Wallpaper Museum in the world is to be found in the Wilhelmshöhe Castle in Kassel. Charging only twelve cents admission, the museum offers an awesome collection of different wallpapers from their earliest beginnings. The most valuable wallpaper on display was made of leather, an art developed in Córdoba, Spain. Another prized wallpaper is the so-called *Flock-Tapete* of the early eighteenth century that consists of bronzed linen on which wool dust has been blown. Showing a wide range of artistic wall decorations, the museum has the famous "Amor and Psyche" wallpaper made in 1810 by Dufour in Paris.

For people with other tastes, the Soup Museum in Baden-Württemberg has over 45,000 soup recipes from all over the world which visitors may copy. Equally as compelling for gourmet types is the Bread Museum in Ulm. Founded in 1955, this free museum displays hundreds of differently shaped loaves of bread from many countries (all stale) and has on view baking utensils of all kinds, some of which go back to Roman times.

Because Germany is full of people who could not resist the temptation to display the objects of their hobbies, it should not come as a surprise to learn that there are museums devoted entirely to tin soldiers (at Kulmbach), to violins (Mittenwald), to tobacco (Buende), to beer (Munich), to horses (Verden an der Aller) and to torture. One of Germany's most eye-arresting museums is the one filled entirely with medieval torture instruments. What even makes this one more unusual is that the museum rooms used to be the actual torture chambers of the small Franconian town of Rothenburg ob der Tauber. Crammed with gadgets and machines of almost unimaginable description, the museum rooms are in a weather-worn Gothic building near the main outer wall that rings the tiny town.

The torture gadgets consist of thumbscrews, racks, pliers for yanking out tongues, iron handcuffs and ankle shackles (their inner surfaces still dotted with spikes), burning irons, a stretching ladder, skull crackers and a large foot-shaped container in which the victim's foot was doused with boiling oil or molten lead. One of the most devilish instruments is that used in the old days to chasten women who gossiped about others, an iron collar with a protruding bar in back. It was affixed around the necks of talkative women who were fastened to a wall in the market square to be taunted by passersby.

In contrast, Germany's happiest museum is the Schnapps Museum of Hindorf which has a collection of nearly four thousand bottles—all filled. This museum shows two hundred different brands of rum, one hundred French cognacs and fifty-two original vodkas, not to mention wines and liqueurs that are well over a century old. Unlike any other museum, this place is prepared to sell some of its showcase items to visitors. Anybody who wants to sample a drink is welcome. There is only one catch. Prices start at fifty dollars a jigger.

117

Author Nino Lo Bello
demonstrates umbrella
composer Richard Wagner invented
(PHOTO BY IRENE ROONEY LO BELLO).

KURIOSA
UND KITSCH

A VIRTUALLY UNKNOWN FACT about Richard Wagner, the bigger-than-life German composer [1813–1883], is that he invented an umbrella to end, he thought, all umbrellas. The strange-looking umbrella is on public view for the first time in Bayreuth's newly opened Richard Wagner Museum, together with a crushing array of Wagneriana and several thousand other musical memorabilia that make Villa Wahnfried (in which the music magician lived his last ten years) dessert for anybody who feasts on Wagner's operas here.

Yes, during the entire year and not only in the summer when the Bayreuth Festival is on, the ghost of Wagner takes morning and early afternoon bows as he does a daily encore in the Museum. Through some twenty rooms, wander and fill yourself to your heart's content on the Wagner archives that have been carefully laid out in chronological order and in logical categories. Take that umbrella of his, for instance. . . .

The umbrella is to be found in a small first-floor chamber called "Kuriosa, Kitsch und Kostbarkeiten." Having always complained about getting one shoulder wet under a standard um-

118

brella, Wagner invented one that pleased him. He replaced the usual handle with a double one so that the carrier's face would be in the central focal point with the V's arms on either side of the head. Apparently no umbrella company ever saw fit to reproduce Wagner's brainstorm of what an umbrella should be like, so the one he personally constructed and used graces the Museum today as perhaps his biggest failure.

The Museum also contains other Wagnerian treasures that are bound to sponge up all your time, happily, on the day you visit. There are, for example, Wagner's own library of 2,281 books, the original handwritten scores of eight of his works, 11,000 letters, notes and memos, his death mask, a plaster cast of his right hand, the sofa on which he died, all his furniture, his pianos, his butterfly collection and the complete correspondence between himself and King Ludwig II, the neurotic Bavarian castle-builder who depleted the state treasury to build Wagner his Bayreuth Festival House.

Together with his pet dog, Wagner himself is buried next to his wife Cosima in a small grove of trees and bushes in back of the Villa. She, the daughter of Franz Liszt and the wife of the conductor-pianist Hans von Bülow, was wooed away from her husband by Wagner (who was also Bülow's best friend) and bore him three children. When she died in 1930 at age 92, she was buried alongside Wagner.

Wagner's heirs now run the annual summer festival, and although they have had their public differences in the past, they were unanimous on one issue. When the Wagner archives were offered for sale in 1970, the material heritage of the great man was to remain in Bayreuth intact and made available to researchers and to his legion of worshipers. When the West German government outbid everyone else for the collection and paid close to three million dollars for them in 1973, it was understood that eventually the empty Villa Wahnfried would be converted into a Richard Wagner Museum.

One important item is still missing from the Museum, however. When the cornerstone of the Festival House was laid, Wagner put a metal box with some of his "secrets" into the concrete giving orders that it not be opened until a hundred years after his death. Music historians and Wagner buffs are waiting impatiently for that day, which falls due in 1983.

Stocked with plenty of grist for the mill, the Museum is expected to attract better than 100,000 visitors a year. The Richard Wagner Museum is open seven days a week from 9 a.m. till 5:00, except on December 24 and 25, January 1 and Easter Sunday.

Taped stereo concerts of Wagner's music (who else?) are given several times a day in the Museum's main auditorium, where free daily lectures are also given during July and August to explain the same evening's particular opera, together with illustrative excerpts.

Since Bayreuth now has a Museum that bulges with the sight and sound of The Man, the euphoric disciples of Wagner today have a second holy sanctum to worship their one true music god everlastingly. The Absolute Being of Bayreuth would have nodded approval because each one of the Museum rooms is in tune with the harmonious language of Richard Wagner. This would have indeed been music to his ears.

119

THE WONDERFUL WALLS OF BREMEN

TOURISTIC ONE-UPMANSHIP has its ups and downs—you win one, you lose one. So it goes. But if you are looking for something that is on the up-and-up and want to be one step ahead of everyone with a photo or color slide that will upstage everybody else's picture collection, then lug your camera and self to Germany's oldest seaport.

Bremen houses two of Northern Europe's most improbable sights—even your wide-angle lens will be wide-eyed at what you're shooting. Optical illusions to the contrary, in different parts of this bustling port city—but within a twenty minute walk of each other—you'll find two buildings with gigantic murals outside, guaranteed to bring a smile to your face, assuming you believe what you see. Really now, how many people ever take a picture of a picture?

What you see is what you get when you go to the corner of Leipziger Strasse and Magdeburger Strasse in Bremen's residential Findorff neighborhood. There you find a Brobdingnagian painting that covers the whole side of what was once a bare, ugly wall of a building that used to be a Nazi bunker and is now a warehouse. Rather than keep a gray brick wall as an unattractive front, in 1975 the owner commissioned an artist to paint on it.

Brush-magician Erich Grams, a pensioned miner in his mid-fifties, took on the four-story structure. He created an illusion that the house lacked one wall and that, in eight rooms on four floors, various domestic activities were taking place, all in a magnificent perspective that might have made Leonardo da Vinci kelly green with envy. It all looks like some kind of comic strip, and certainly no art critic would ever classify the mural or any of its panels as "art." Whether it's art or not, it interests you nonetheless.

One scene shows a family of four at the dinner table, another a quartet of young persons involved in a ping pong match, a third a group of children busy in a playroom with a blackboard full of scrawl in the background and a window at the side through which trees and sky are visible. Laundry hangs in the top floor room, which is flanked by a man who is building a brick wall that would presumably cover up all the eight exposed rooms.

Eliciting the most comment is the segment on the third floor which shows a young man on a swing with his legs spread-eagled. Swinging toward you, he seems to be coming right out of the house onto the street, because his feet appear to be sticking out past the wall. The effect is great.

In another part of town, about five minutes from the main railroad station in a traffic circle at the end of Rembertiring road, you will find Bremen's other al fresco work of art. An unidentified artist has done up a picture of an elderly couple sitting at their front window and taking in the street sights.

Actually, the building is an old folks' home in what otherwise would be considered a drab part of town. Without doubt, the large painting that occupies the whole wall adds a bit of zest to the scenery. Nearby residents tell you that the perfect couple at the window are quiet neighbors—they never gossip, never borrow a cup of sugar and never complain about the noisy children next door.

Bremen, however, is not the only city in Germany today that has house paintings out front. Obliquely referred to as "the wall game," the outside murals have become a kind of craze today and, where private homeowners are not commissioning artists to decorate houses, city governments throughout Germany have been contracting painters to dress up buildings. West Berlin's zoo has a huge wall called "The World Tree" that needed three artists to do. The city of Altona has decorated its railroad terminal with an exterior diorama that looks like a passenger car with people sitting inside, a gimmicky scene that makes you scratch your head. And one factory in Schornstein decorated its facade with a picture of the factory and a chimney blowing thick industrial smoke. This is one smokestack that doesn't pollute.

The craze for exterior house-painting started about six years ago when Erich Grams painted his own house in Karlshausen after retiring. He didn't know what he was starting when he created a fantasy landscape of birds, beasts and flowers. When the colorful mural brought on squawks from his neighbors and even a lawsuit, which he won, Grams became a minor celebrity of a sort as hundreds of rubberneckers from all around flocked to his house daily to sightsee. Soon people and city governments all over the country were offering him money to dandify their buildings. First to admit he's not even a mini-Rembrandt, Grams says almost apologetically: "If I can bring a smile to a few faces where drab colors dominate a street, then I feel my work has some value." He says he'd like to try his hand on Wall Street.

Wall painting in Bremen.

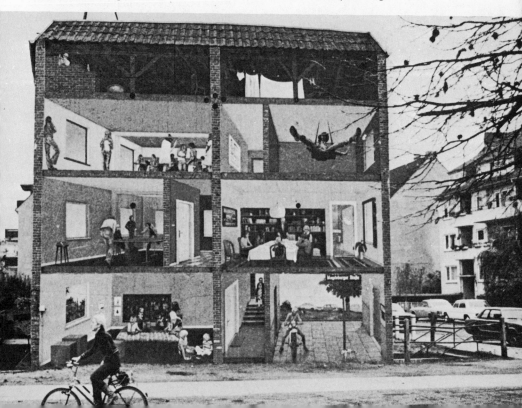

*Beers from many countries of the world
at this unusual inn
near Munich.*

THE HOUSE OF
101 BEERS

THROUGHOUT HISTORY it's been known by such endearing names as nipitatum, huff-cap, stingo, Pharaoh, mum, lager and bier. Brewed with barley, hops and water, the thirst-quenching stuff that is the world's favorite drink has now become a unique tourist attraction in The House of 101 Beers in Starnberg, a town fifteen miles south of Munich.

The world's largest collection of un-

usual beers from twenty-four countries is to be found at the edge of town in a quaint Bavarian inn that features golden brews from as far away as Red China and Australia and from such unexpected places as Africa and Iceland. The House of 101 Beers actually keeps in stock and on tap, by official count, somewhere between 130 and 135 different beers, most of which, understandably, are from Germany.

122

Contrary to expectations, the one country missing from the inn's imposing lineup is the United States. According to proprietor Artidoro Allodi, a 45-year-old Italian from Milan who took over the inn ten years ago, American beers never pass Germany's strict brewing laws, which go back to the year 1516, because of "their chemical content."

"I'm not allowed to import or sell American beers," Mr. Allodi explains, "because the companies use artificial preservatives of one kind or another, and therefore don't pass the government laboratory tests. I'm hoping a U.S. company will brew up a special beer just for me, for export to Germany only, one that would get by our tough brewing laws."

Which are some of the inn's unusual beers?

Apart from the standard assortment, which runs the gamut of "light beer" (heavy on the hops and light on the malt) to "dark beer" (with more malt content and less hops), The House of 101 Beers carries some odd brews. That would include "oyster beer" from Ireland; "smoked beer" from Poland, which has a flavor like ham; and the world's only beer that is alcohol free—it is also very low in calories.

"As you might have guessed, my bestselling beer, month in and month out, is from Communist China. It's an okay beer in my book but not one of my personal favorites. Tourists ask for it mostly out of curiosity, but some of my regular customers actually order it regularly," says Allodi.

Two German types that he keeps in stock have special distinctions among the world's beers. One is a beer from Kulmbach, which is "the strongest beer in the world," because it has the highest alcoholic content (28 per cent). The other is "the world's most expensive beer." Coming in an odd-shaped small bottle that has a printed serial number on it and is sealed with a thick circle of red wax, this particular beer is from a brewery in Treuchtlingen, which was founded in 1516, and which matures the beer for seven years in special temperature-controlled cellars before sending it out to market.

Though offering a complete menu of gourmet dishes and providing hotel lodging, The House of 101 Beers does a tidy business on the sale of glasses and mugs that go with certain brands. Many regular customers, however, have their own steins with their names imprinted thereon; these are kept on the shelf in a chronological order based on how long a client has been a regular.

The special glasses and mugs on sale are ones that have been designed by the breweries and display a brewery's crest or some kind of quaint identification. One type of North Bavarian beer from Wagner's festival town of Bayreuth is always dispensed in a special pewter tankard, whereas all Polish beers are served in a high V-shaped glass.

Allodi considers himself an expert on beer glasses. Before pouring beer into a glass, it should be rinsed in cold water, thereby removing any odors, especially cigarette smell, that may be clinging to it. As for the washing of glasses, he recommends using a sudsless detergent and draining them dry. Never wipe a beer glass because the touch of most towels is enough to make it unsatisfactory later for serving beer. Lipstick, by the way, is a beer glass' big enemy.

But, according to Allodi, women are often beer's biggest enemy, as far as beer-lovers are concerned. "Can you imagine someone not drinking a glass of beer but using it either as a base for stew or as a hair rinse?"

GERMANY'S "KANSAS CITY"

FROM NORTH BAVARIA, according to most maps, Kansas City is some four thousand miles away. But the "Kansas City" in Plech, North Bavaria (the one in quotation marks) is a hop, skip and a five-mile jump from Nuremberg. West Germany's "Kansas City," however, is strictly a cowboy town. You won't see Wild Bill Hickok

"Kansas City" in Germany.

acomin' down Main Street, but you will see Mayor Franz Schmitt or his sidekick, storekeeper Wilhelm Nette, hitching up their gunbelts and greeting you with a friendly teutonic, "Howdy, *mein Herr!"*

Practically in the shadow of Wagner's festival town of Bayreuth, the Old West has been recreated in lookee-here style by a forty-eight-year-old farmer, Sheriff Ernst Schuster, a cuss who packs a six-gun, too, and sports a tilted ten-gallon hat. His hobby since he was knee-high to a chuck wagon has been the frontier days of America and the legendary cowpokes who shot their way to distinction and extinction.

In the summer of 1977, fulfilling a long-cherished dream, Sheriff Schuster opened up his own idea of a *"Wunderland,"* Western style, complete with a hangman's rope, a choochoo train and station, a typical cowpunchers' saloon (it serves whisky and bratwurst), a sheriff's office with two jail cells, an ole corral, and an operating gold mine unit where people can do their panning for nuggets. The nearby Western Club of

Nuremberg hies over to "Kansas City" on Sundays to put on two afternoon shows, which are highlighted by a "High Noon" shoot-out.

Visitors to "Kansas City" can board a stagecoach and go for an authentic bumpy (emphasis on the bumpy) ride around the countryside. There is also a bareback riding range and a shooting gallery with real Winchesters. For a small coin, you can take a trip on a choochoo that is a mini-copy of one from the old Atchison, Topeka & Santa Fe Line, which will take you around the town in several huffs and into the wooded area nearby in several puffs. Any moment you are, mebbe, expecting to meet up with Gary Cooper or Randolph Scott.

In the homey saloon, the bartender dispenses whisky and/or beer (even Cokes for tenderfoots) and, if you want some grub, there is plenty of bratwurst and sauerkraut on hand, plus other assorted vittles like ham sandwiches and popcorn.

Other attractions include a blacksmith shop, a cemetery of Dodge City tombstones with epitaphs, a public stock (into which you can insert your wrists and have yourself photographed as a public offender), an Indian camp with real teepees, a ranch house with fenced-in cattle, and a Pony Express hotel with at least ten bunks for folks who get a hankering for some overnight shuteye.

Anybody who wants to pan for gold nuggets can do so free of charge at the operating gold mine unit at the edge of town where an attendant (who looks like Walter Brennan without makeup) explains how you can do it the way the boys back then used to. There is no guarantee you'll find any real gold, however, unless some one happens to have lost his or her wedding band the day before.

"Kansas City" is the second section of a three-section fun setup. The first part, completed in 1976, is a kiddie play park where Junior can meet up with Hansel and Gretel, Little Red Riding Hood, *et al.*, among an array of toys, gadgets, gimmicks and playground apparatus to delight even the big folks. For the third section, Sheriff Schuster is afixin' to attach a "Dinosaurland" so that the kids can see what real dinosaurs and tyrannosaurs looked like, critters the Wild West never really had on the range.

Working closely with Sheriff Schuster is an American citizen varmint, a storekeeper who runs the Wild West souvenir shop. German-born Billy Nette (who changed his name from Wilhelm after living in New York City for twenty-five years) and his wife Anni (now Anne, she packs a mean six-gun herself and can draw faster than Billy the Kid) are ready to greet all strangers who breeze into town. With a palaver that's real purty-like, Nette and his squaw dispense any info you kinda like to have in English.

Schuster's children are also helping out. Bedecked in her maxi pioneer dress, lovely Monika, nineteen years old, watches over the "Kansas City" bank (posing on request for any tourist's camera), twenty-year-old Rita takes care of the finances and the playground, and Ernst Jr., fourteen, is a deputy sheriff in charge of "public relations." Hooking a thumb in his worn gunbelt, he sez he likes to meet up with any hombre who moseys into town. Hi-yo Silver and Donnerwetter! This is one cowboy town Wyatt Earp would never savvy, especially if he got a load of the soft ice cream machine down yonder by the ole corral. The city slicker who runs it calls it Custard's Last Stand.

125

IF YOU'RE A TRIVIA quiz buff, here's a travel question to test your knowledge. Frankenstein's Castle is (check one):

(a) the name of Boris Karloff's home.

(b) non-existent and strictly fiction.

(c) to be found in West Germany.

The correct answer is (c). But if you insist that Frankenstein's Castle, which everyone knows wasn't the name of Boris Karloff's home, is non-existent and strictly fiction, then come to this central Germany town of Nieder-Beerbach, a few miles beyond the city limits of Darmstadt. You'll find said Castle all right, right here in the middle of the woods but . . . er, you won't find the Monster or the ghost of Frankenstein.

Still, Frankenstein's Castle is one of the most tempting tourist attractions in all Germany today, judging from the way the Germans themselves flock to visit it each year. As you might expect, the castle—looking like something out of a nightmare—is perched on a narrow ridge amid some steep enveloping woods.

What may shake the whole image, however, is that when you finally reach the celebrated bastion on foot, you discover an ultramodern restaurant with a menu pushing its house specialty: "Spit-Roasted Pork à la Castle Frankenstein." In addition to private dining facilities "ideal for business conferences and wedding receptions," the restaurant even has streamlined guest rooms where you can book an overnight stay.

If this is not quite Frankensteinish enough, then you can always sit on the cafe terrace, nurse a cup of teutonic java with whipped cream, bask in the glorious view of the surrounding wooded countryside and give multiple looks at the enticing ruins that go back to the pages of medieval German history.

Because there isn't a movie fan anywhere who hasn't seen "Frankenstein" at least once, local historians would love to tell the world, but are a bit baffled, how Frankenstein Castle came to provide the setting for a novel written in 1818 by Mary Wollstonecraft Shelley. Though not documented, it's believed that Mrs. Shelley visited Frankenstein Castle on a trip through Germany and then simply "borrowed" it for her horror novel. She also borrowed the name Frankenstein for her ghoulish grave-robbing baron.

One German scholar advances the view that the fictional Baron Frankenstein might have been based on a man who did indeed exist. He was an offbeat human being by the name of Johann Konrad Dippel, born in the castle in 1673, who later earned some notoriety as an alchemist. A loner who would often walk about with his nose stuck in a book or read in the tower by candlelight late into the night, Dippel was forever conducting experiments, mostly to discover how to make gold or figure out "what the secret of life was."

His weird testing included boiling bones and hair and heating them at various temperatures with iron flecks and dried blood clots. One of his formulas led to the discovery of the deadly Prussic acid poison. While usually secretive about his work, Dippel once bragged he could prolong life, but he died without putting the methodology down on paper. He did, however, invent a blue textile dye still in use.

Erected in the year 1252, the starkly

forbidding fortification originally belonged to Conrad von Frankenstein. He built it because, as a Catholic, he did not want to get mixed up in an endless feud, a lifestyle in those days, with his hostile Protestant neighbors. Over the stretch of time, the feudal stronghold underwent major modifications so that the ruin today represents architectural facelift attempts running from the hodge of the Middle Ages through the podge of the seventeenth century. If nothing else, it looks today exactly like what a Hollywood film castle is supposed to look like—spooky and desolate, especially on a foggy day—which is why in 1931 Universal Pictures adopted it as a model and backdrop for the celebrated Boris Karloff film.

Actor Boris Karloff, who played the Frankenstein monster with macabre perfection and who made a career of scaring people on the screen, visited the castle here shortly before his death. Whether he was fascinated or not, he never said, but he did leave behind the following remark: "It's a place for goose pimples, but the only thing chilling about it is the draft inside."

Frankenstein Castle.

Dorotheum.

THE WORLD'S BIGGEST PAWNSHOP

BETWEEN ENERGY-DRAINING performances of heavy opera, Swedish soprano Birgit Nilsson likes nothing better when in the Austrian capital than to hie off to the world's biggest pawnshop and auctioneering establishment, situated in the shadow of the Vienna Staatsoper, and watch the greatest show on earth.

So do a lot of other people. Maybe that is why the Dorotheum draws the Viennese like flies to honey. Unfortunately, ever so few tourists poke curious noses into the Dorotheum, but that can be blamed on the standard travel guides which rarely bother to tip the tourist off about one of the most fascinating places anywhere.

Established more than 265 years ago by Emperor Josef I, the Dorotheum is a place in which all tourists should get lost. In fact, Dorotheum officials are sometimes reluctant to admit it, but unconfirmed reports indicate there may still be people wandering around its as yet uncounted rooms who stopped in for a peek during the reign of Napoleon.

The Dorotheum is located at Number 17 Dorotheergasse, a curvy, alley-like street in the heart of town. Admission is free to the vast pawn and loan house, but once inside you quickly become aware in no uncertain terms that you will open your purse because facing you is a shopper's paradise, the hugest showcase in the world. Controlled by the Ministry of the Interior as a charitable institution, the Dorotheum keeps on display every imaginable commodity, ranging from an abacus owned by an abbot to a zither used by a Zulu. Casually wander among the scores of rooms, up and down who knows how many staircases, and feast your eyes on more than umpteen zillion used items which soon become grist for the auctioneer's gavel.

Besides granting pawn loans at the lowest rates of interest to be found in Europe, the Dorotheum serves as a middleman in the acquisition and sale of objects. Nine or ten auctions take place almost every day in various segments of the Dorotheum and you had better go early if you want a seat or even standing room. Unless you plan to acquire something, it is better to attend without money for, after watching the proceedings, it is almost impossible to resist temptation (for some Viennese, it's almost a disease!). You don't even need to know German—just raise your hand or nod your head and you may find yourself the sudden owner of a lampshade that might have belonged to Johann Strauss' third wife. That is what makes the Dorotheum.

Taking place several times a year, the big art auctions usually draw connoisseurs and dealers from all over Europe. Not long ago, one art ignoramus struck it lucky when he bought a grimy oil painting which turned out to be a Goya. An antique dealer from the provinces once bid and got for pennies a musty folder which contained sixteen drawings by the Austrian master, Gustav Klimt, each worth thousands of dollars.

Allied bombs wreaked heavy havoc on the Dorotheum during the war and what remained was just a skeleton. But the Austrians were determined to rebuild their fabulous secondhand shop which they have nicknamed, *"Die Tante Dorothee"* ("Aunt Dorothy"). Faced with an almost impossible job, Dorotheum employees pitched in and helped with the shoveling, carted away debris and did the final clean-up. In April 1945, the main building was reopened amid holiday ceremonies.

Every year the Dorotheum stages some four thousand auctions for which nearly a million and a half sundry objects are placed on exhibit. Annually these things bring in from bidders better than four million dollars in profit from the charges of up to twenty percent the Dorotheum exacts on each transaction. Because the jumbo hock shop is a non-profit institution, all of the money that is earned, over and above expenses, is required by law to be applied towards lowering the interest rates on pawned items and on loans to the poor.

What draws the crowds day after day to the Dorotheum, however tourist-neglected it may be, is the strikingly low price at which the bidding is pegged to start on many items. Build a better mousetrap and the world will beat a path to the door. Or do what "Tante Dorothee" does: Sell the mousetrap instead—and people will build a path to your store.

AUSTRIA'S PIXILATED LAKE

IN DEFIANCE OF ALL rules of hydrography, Austria hosts a lake—the third largest in Europe—which is so full of peculiarities that baffled geography professors jokingly say the psychologists ought to be the ones analyzing the pond's schizophrenic characteristics and sundry psychoneuroses.

The tourist coming to Vienna who has a thirst for the oddest at work would do well to leave the Danube capital for a morning's jaunt southeastward to the Burgenland and its mysterious Neusiedler See, the twenty-two mile long pixilated steppelake which is surrounded by a thick belt of reeds and which beats anything yet. Charmed with its array of idiosyncracies, a dedicated offtrail wanderer will not solve the mystery of Austria's Neusiedler See, but he will certainly delight in the double dose of Agatha Christie and the double dash of Robert Ripley that the Neusiedler See dishes up.

The first fact about the big puddle, which is less than an hour's drive from midtown Vienna, is that, since the beginning of recorded time, it has completely disappeared once every hundred years—and nobody knows why! Every time the lake erases itself from the map, the inhabitants of the adjoining villages reopen the disputes and lawsuits from the century before as to who owns the carefully measured and staked-out parcels of flatland lake bed. Then the lawyers and litigants squabble with each other and, as the costs of the legal action soar, all of a sudden the water pocket reappears without any fanfare and reoccupies its original area as if nothing had happened. That quiets down all the court fuss—until the next century.

But the erratic personality of the Neusiedler See, which was once the bottom of an inland ocean that vanished a thousand years ago, does not stop there. There is the fact that no one knows where its waters come from or why the water is salty and not sweet. The Wulka is the only river that flows into it. But the Wulka is really more of a rivulet and geographers who measure the 124 square miles of aquatic split personality have discovered that the lake loses four times as much water through normal evaporation than what the Wulka pours in. Additionally, the Burgenland's body of water has a habit of rising and falling so that sometimes it is three feet deep straight across and other times it is six feet deep. Occasionally, without warning, the loony lake gets a yen to overflow its low banks and swallows up some of the lakeside communities—during a dry spell!

Contributing to the peculiarities is a one-directional wind from the plains that buffets the lake so that very often nearly all the water rolls up into the farthest west corner. This one-directional wind, known as the *"Windstau,"* is a hazard to sailboaters and has caused some drownings. But it does not seem to ruffle the remarkable herons and exotic fauna which use the wavy jungle of sighing reeds as their nesting places. There are over 250 different species of rare aquatic fowl, such as the bearded titmouse, the egret, the willow-wren and the bustard, leading a freebooter's life in this richly stocked feathered sanctuary.

To add to the lake's kookiness, there is the Cold War; a small part of the lake is Communist. At its eastern end, the Hungarian-Austrian border runs zigzag across the Neusiedler See and, while swimming is rarely dangerous in the low waters, a bather who inadvertently paddles too close to Hungary can find himself mixed up with an armed Communist patrol boat or the target of a nervous Red machinegun tower.

The Burgenlanders tell a touching folktale of a creature known as Wasserstoffel who lived in the Neusiedler See in the form of a human being with the habits of a fish. He was caught and tamed. But, at a wedding feast, he came with a dubious gift—a sackful of marine insects, his idea of a table delicacy. This wedding present did not quite go over well, and Wasserstoffel slinked off into the lake, never to be seen again. It is this mixed-up Neusiedler See character, say the locals, who has mixed up the character of the Neusiedler See.

Dock facilities
at the Rust side of
Austria's Neusiedler Lake
(PHOTO BY IRENE ROONEY LO BELLO).

DRIVE YOUR OWN CHOOCHOO

QUICK NOW, where can a tourist go who's a real, dyed-in-the-wool railroad buff if he wants to drive a choochoo train himself?

Well, he can go where the action is, to Murau in the scenic Mur Valley in the middle of Austria and, for a small fee, he can climb into the engineer's cab, place himself at the controls and drive a real steam locomotive to his heart's content.

Mind you, the Mur Valley's amateur locomotive (known in German as the Murtalbahn Amateurlok) is not in any sense a kiddie railroad running on a set of toy tracks for big folks. Not at all. The steam horse you drive is the real McCoy; you have a number of railroad cars attached, including a dining car with a bar; and you chug along the regular tracks that all the other commercial passenger and freight trains use. Kid stuff it isn't!

For a small fee any person can climb into the cab of this choochoo and drive the train over ninety miles of track (PHOTO BY IRENE ROONEY LO BELLO).

Even if you're *not* careful, you couldn't have a crack-up because the Mur Valley Railroad provides you with a professional fireman in the cab and, while he stokes the flames and keeps the steam at the proper pressure, he has an expert eye peeled to see you don't pull any boo-boos as you blissfully puff along.

The Mur Valley Line runs about ninety miles and makes the trip in about two and a half hours through some of the most majestic lowland and hill country you've ever seen, making stops at Mauterndorf, Murau (the main station and headquarters of the line) and Unzmarkt. You do, nevertheless, pass by the towns of Tamsweg, Predlitz, Teufenbach, Stadl, Niederwölz and Scheifling and, in each of these locales, if you give a sporting toot on your whistle, you'll get a friendly Austrian wave back.

Any would-be Casey Jones who wants to get in on this once in a lifetime deal has only to write in advance to reserve a time and a day. You can book the iron mule in fifteen minute segments or rent it for as many hours as your pocketbook can stand. But you must fit your departure into the scheduled timetable of the regular trains that come and go during the day.

Two steam engines are available for hire. The bigger "U.43" locomotive, built in 1913, rents for forty dollars an hour, while the smaller "U.40" locomotive, built in 1909, rents for twenty-eight dollars an hour. If you bring your family along to ride in the passenger cars, each member has only to pay the regular fare.

"There's a dining car attached," explains Harald Grafinger, assistant director of the Mur Valley Line (to whom inquiries can be addressed), "and you pay only what you order in the way of drinks or snacks. We provide a waiter at no additional expense. And I might mention there's no charge for the fireman on duty. He will give advice and instructions to the amateur engineer at no cost whatever."

So far, since the "amateur engineer" program was started in 1969, there have been no wrecks whatever. Already the Line has drawn innumerable railroad buffs who now come each year (a few even several times a year) to hit the cinder trail. Even tourists from as far away as Japan and Canada come for a run. Every fan who drives the locomotive receives an engraved certificate, suitable for framing.

Last year the Murtalbahn even had a sheikh from the Middle East operate the controls. Once, Italian tenor Giuseppe Di Stefano tried his hand at the throttle and the folks who waved at him noted that he kept his whistle in perfect pitch. Said Engineer Di Stefano: "What a feeling of importance you get up front passing all those autos lined up at the crossings!"

The Mur Valley Line doesn't seem to get many women wanting to drive a train, according to Grafinger. "But we have noticed that the fans who sit at the controls tend to drive faster than our regular engineers. I ought to mention that the 'U.43' has a speed limit of twenty-four miles per hour, whereas the 'U.40' can only go fifteen miles an hour."

Although there are no tunnels on the Line, the railroad boasts of having what is the only bridge in Europe that has a curved track on it—which can be a bit dangerous if negotiated at full speed. But then your fire-stoking sidekick in the big teakettle will brief you properly on that particular stretch. Do what the man tells you because he is only trying to train you.

THE MOUSE THAT BELLOWED

Tiny chapel at Oberndorf, Austria, where "Silent Night" was played for the first time (PHOTO BY DIETRICH).

IT WOULD BE HARD to find Oberndorf on the map of Austria, but you can thank a mouse that people pay homage here to the greatest Christmas carol of them all. For if the busy little rodent had not been the mouse that bellowed, perhaps "Silent Night" would never have spread all over the world.

134

Contrary to what is sometimes believed, that "Stille Nacht" (the German title for "Silent Night") was written by Haydn's younger brother, the famed Yuletide song had its origins in this tiny town of three thousand near the German-Austrian border not far from Salzburg. The St. Nicholas church, where the Christmas song was played and sung for the first time over 150 years ago, is no longer standing but the proud Austrians have erected a memorial chapel here where the church once stood as a kind of monument to the immortal tune. At Christmastime, tourists come from all over Europe to the "Silent Night Chapel" to hear a performance of "Stille Nacht" they will never forget. But nobody remembers the mouse anymore. Alas. . . .

"Silent Night" was born of a collaboration between a Catholic priest, Joseph Mohr, who wrote the words and a schoolmaster, Franz Xavier Gruber, composer-organist for the Oberndorf church, who wrote the music. After creating hundreds of musical pieces, Gruber died in 1863 at the age of seventy-five, but nothing he composed had the lasting value of the unassuming little theme he wrote for a Christmas concert in 1818.

Because a hungry mouse had chewed a hole in the leather bellows of his organ, Gruber could not give his annual Yuletide organ concert. But Father Mohr had an idea. Having written several verses of a Christmas poem, he asked Gruber to put these to music so that, on Christmas Eve, instead of an organ recital, the church could do a choral performance. Entitled simply "Christmas Song," Gruber's new piece was sung for the first time by the voices of dozens of villagers with a long guitar accompaniment. It was years later that "Christmas Song" became "Stille Nacht." The song would no doubt have quietly fallen into the limbo of forgotten melodies if fate had not somehow shaped its destiny.

To get the mouse-gnawed bellows repaired, Gruber called in Karl Mauracher, a well-known organ builder from the Tyrol. As part of his payment for putting the organ back into shape, Mauracher was given a copy of the new ditty to take home with him. Unaware of the impact it would have, the organ mender showed the Christmas hymn to some of his clients who recopied it for a try on their own organs. One of these extra copies apparently fell into the hands of a group of Tyrolean glovemakers, the Strassers, who used to travel all over Germany selling their wares at local fairs. To attract buyers to their booth, the Strasser Sisters used to sing Austrian songs, one of which was Gruber's little air. Only in the year 1831 did the song click, however. That happened at the Leipzig Fair when the Strassers' warbling of "Stille Nacht" caught the fancy of the Duke of Leipzig. Impressed, he invited the singing sisters to visit his court and present it for his guests.

But the best song-plugger of them all was King William I of Prussia. He adored the carol and later, as Emperor of Germany, urged it be played during the year-end feasting, both in the Protestant north as well as in the Catholic south. Though other tunes in our modern times have become famous overnight, eventually they drop out of sight. But not "Silent Night." We can thank fate for keeping Gruber's beloved masterpiece alive. . . . and mighty mouse for getting into the groove.

THE WORLD'S MOST ECCENTRIC VALLEY

SUPPOSE WE CALL it the world's most eccentric valley. Breathes there a tourist who can match it with anything like it in his travels?

Klein Walsertal is part of Austria but you cannot enter the valley from Austria. There is no direct route because it is shut off from the rest of Austria by a U-shaped wall of insurpassable mountains and ridges so you have to make a round the mulberry bush trip into West Germany and come in that way through the town of Oberstdorf. Even more surprising is the fact that in Klein Walsertal Austrian goods are subject to import duties, while German goods move in free. Yet the people who live in the Walsertal are ruled by Austrian laws, vote in Austrian elections and pay Austrian taxes. The inhabitants here, moreover, are of Swiss origin but the language they speak does not resemble other Austrian or German dialects and is virtually incomprehensible to the Swiss.

The comic-opera situation in the Walsertal is a rib-tickler to most visitors, but not to the Austrians. Wryly, they sometimes refer to it as "Austria's only colony." Citizens from the "Austrian mainland" who want to go slumming and pay a tourist call to the valley with the split personality find even another surprise in store for them. To their chagrin, they learn that in many shops Austrian schillings are not accepted. Thus, though they are on Austrian soil, Austrian citizens still have to convert their native money at the bank into German marks to make purchases. The Walsertalians prefer to trade with German money because,

they argue, it has always been done that way so why bother changing over and complicating things even more.

This curious circumstance came about as a result of an agreement concluded in 1891 between statesmen of the two countries. Because the valley could only be entered through Germany, one of the things decided was that German customs officers should have the responsibility of controlling the frontier. But, across the border, law and order are maintained by Austrian police. Also add to Klein Walsertal's curiosities the fact that the postal trucks which serve "Austria's only colony" are German, but the stamps on the letters are Austrian, payable in German marks. However, both countries apply the same postal rates for letters going into and coming out of Klein Walsertal.

To put an end to the turvy-topsy situation, Austria's authorities are considering building a road so that the thirty-eight square miles of isolated never-never land can be tied umbilically to the home grounds. Just recently, an antenna was installed on a nearby peak so now, for the first time, the locals can watch Austrian television. Pleased with the new television setup, the proud people who have been living here for centuries (today's population is about four thousand) nevertheless say they do not want a new state highway that would link them with the other side of the mountain. They prefer the *status* to remain *quo*.

For tourists who want to go through the fuss of getting here, the fuss is less than it seems, provided you do not start

*Main street of Riezlern,
capital of Klein Walsertal.*

from Austria. The valley is about sixty miles from the German shore of Lake Constance and a little over one hundred miles southwest of Munich. Klein Walsertal is not listed on many maps, so you would have to look hard at a good one.

The sleepy lowland was at one time used by Western Austria's noble families for hunting but, when hardy settlers from the Swiss canton of Valais filtered in during the fourteenth century, it became farmland. Now Klein Walsertal shares in the ski boom. Each of the three villages sharing the valley is well-equipped to cater to the ski crowd. They are Riezlern, Hirschegg and Mittelberg-Baad, which blend in symphonic harmony with the *coda* of magnificent Alpine peaks. In any of Klein Walsertal's hamlets, a visitor can find lodging in a farmhouse for as little as two dollars a day including breakfast or for nine dollars a day with three meals in one of the color-slide hotels. Klein Walsertal is one of Austria's biggest travel bargains—payable in German money.

137

THE TOWN
THAT DID NOT DIE

A DOG BARKS. Three geese waddle in a fenced backyard. The postman goes by. A housewife hangs up some wash. Two little boys are digging a hole with tablespoons. An old man sits on his porch in a rocking chair, a book opened on his lap as he slumbers. All is peace in Lidice.

Suddenly a dozen overpoweringly loud microphones shatter the air. It is the Czech national anthem. The husky feminine voice of an announcer burbles out patriotic words as a busload full of tourists pulls up to spill out curious and rubbernecking foreigners who have come to see the site of the most infamous massacre of World War II.

To reconstruct Lidice, which the Nazis wiped off the face of the earth almost forty years ago, Czechoslovakia has spent almost fourteen million dollars, most of which has gone into a new village of model homes housing nearly five hundred people. The government has also set up a memorial garden, the largest of its kind in Europe, in which 29,000 rose bushes donated by thirty-five countries on both sides of the Iron Curtain are kept in bloom.

But for all the lovely flowers that are kept alive here, Lidice reminds you of death. It reminds you of one of the most shameful episodes in the history of man. It reminds you of June 10, 1942. People over the world may have forgotten some of the details of that day—but Lidice, both in name and in fact, stands as a memory unto itself.

Until that fateful June day, Lidice was just a small coal mining town. Then the Nazis decided to make an example of Lidice, calculated to bring the Czech people to their knees. This was in reprisal for the assassination of S.S. Obergruppenführer and General of Police Reinhart Heydrich. Because Heydrich's murderers would not give themselves up, the Nazis selected Lidice at random to retaliate. At midnight they herded every man, woman and child out of their homes and, that morning, a firing squad executed every male of Lidice between the ages of fourteen and eighty-four. In all, 192 men faced the execution rifles. The women and children were forthwith transported to the Ravensbruck concentration camp. Girls under twenty-five were assigned to brothels, while the other women were liquidated in gas chambers and cremated in incinerators. Eighty-two of the ninety-one children were gassed to death. The remaining nine, having passed a "racial test" and placed in German families, came back alive after the war.

The Nazis did not stop there, however. They trucked away all the belongings of the townspeople, drove the cattle off, filled in the village pond, diverted a brook in another direction and burned down every house. When they finished a week later, the spot where Lidice once stood remained only a flat, bare plain. To complete the job, the name of Lidice was erased from all maps, land registers and documents.

But Lidice did not die. Her name flew out to the world. Nations all over adopted her. Miners in England organized a "Lidice Shall Live" campaign and raised funds. Mexico gave the city of San Jeronimo the name of Lidice. A town in Illinois took it. Venezuela erected a suburb called Lidice and countries like Cuba, Peru, Ecuador, Chile, Uruguay, India and Egypt built monuments and named streets in honor of the little village.

Today Lidice is Czechoslovakia's main tourist draw. On the spot of the razed village the nation has erected a massive stone monument under which are buried the 192 firing squad victims, their photographs prominently displayed on each crypt. Nearby, on the very ground where the executions took place, the people have set up a crude wooden cross with a hoop of the original barbed wire behind which the Germans herded their hostages that tragic day.

Anybody with heart gazing at the barbed wire, now rusted, cannot avoid feeling its message to posterity.

THE KINGDOM OF SALT

IT TOOK WORKMEN over a thousand years slaving in the bowels of the earth to give Poland what is perhaps Europe's most underworldly lure, an *Alice in Wonderland* salt mine into which some 800,000 tourists a year gingerly descend via fifty-seven flights of wood steps (399 of them) to wander along several rememberable miles of holes and corridors and caverns and hollows and nooks and pockets that have been gouged into that big lump of subterranean sodium chloride. It's enough to make King Solomon's mines look like an anthole.

The salt mine of Wieliczka, which the Polish government has now converted into a state "museum," boasts eight levels of labyrinths. Only three of these, however, going to a depth of 450 feet, are open to the public. In all there are about 125 miles or so of galleries, impossible to visit all at once, so that the guided tour route is therefore limited to a couple of miles, along which the oldest and most interesting parts can be found.

In this Kingdom of Salt, as it is sometimes called by the Poles, you tramp behind your polylingual, indefatigable guide who leads the way with his power lantern. But be forewarned that you could indeed get lost down there if you don't stick like glue to the retired old salt-worker who ushers you around the opaque sanctum of salt.

Because the miners of yesteryear were a superstitious lot, they took to carving altars, holy effigies and bas-relief scenes out of the salt to ward off any possible evil spirits or bad luck down below. Cut with three-dimensional effects, the salt scenes, most of which deal with Biblical themes, are really works of art—and you have to keep reminding yourself that they are made of NaCl. Perhaps the most beautiful of these are the flight out of Egypt, Jesus before the Pharisees and the Last Supper.

In one of the galleries you wander into a dark chapel dedicated to St. Anthony, fashioned some three centuries ago (1689) in dark green salt rock, the work of a miner called Antoni Kuczkowski. Blurred by the action of dampness over the centuries, the three altars and the religious sculptures give the entire chapel an almost surrealistic shape. Before he became Pope John Paul II, Cracow's archbishop, Cardinal Wojtyla, invariably escorted visiting church dignitaries to this stirring site.

Certainly the most impressionable sight of all is the immense ballroom chamber, whose floor measures 177 by 48 feet and whose gray salt walls are adorned with striking bas-relief sculptures. Hanging from the high ceiling are five mammoth chandeliers (all lit up) which have also been made of crystalline salt. This staggering salon is the work of two brothers, Josef and Tomasz Markowski, and one of the sculptures won them a gold medal at the Paris World Exposition in 1905.

Still another large dugout, a bit more on the modern side, serves as a midway rest center for tourists. It offers a salt souvenir shop, a snack stand, a cafe, a night clubbish bar nook and plenty of chairs, tables and benches for the tired trudger. Adjacent is a tennis court which also doubles as a basketball court and at the far end is a band podium for public concerts or dancing.

Not far away is a movie house with plush seats that are kept covered under plastic sheets when not in use. When you leave this area, you are soon led to the bank of a salty underground lake which formed in the seventeenth century. An immense squared pillar of salt in the middle of the big puddle holds up the ceiling. By using a wooden bridge, you can walk across the water to the pillar, which has a path flanking it on two sides.

After you have been tramping around for upwards of two hours, the guide will give you a choice of returning to the top via an open elevator in the wooden shaft or moving on further into a number of museum grottoes where are displayed oldtime salt mining equipment, medieval treadwheels, a showcase of weird-looking salt-encrusted tools and photos that show how salt was mined in days of yore. Don't pass these up. Fair warning!

One friendly word of advice: the guides will try to give you the heebie-jeebies by telling of Wieliczka's legendary underground dwarfs who kidnap unmindful people going astray from their group. You can take this with a grain of salt.

Salt sculpture in Polish mine.

AN UNUSUAL RAILROAD

WHAT A WAY to run a railroad. . .

The serious-faced little girl in the uniform of a conductor coming around to punch the tickets, while your train chugs its way through the wooded hills of Buda on the "other" side of the Hungarian capital, is eleven years old As the four-car train rumbles into Janoshegy Station, two uniformed boys—one aged ten, the other

Young stationmaster in Hungary salutes departing train.

twelve—emerge from the control room, come to stiff attention on the platform and give the familiar European railroad salute. The engineer in the diesel cab up front, all of fourteen, returns the salute. Later, when it's time for the train to move out, one of the two boys will consult his wristwatch, take the flag from under his arm, fill his lungs with air and yell out an authoritative "All a-b-o-a-r-d!!!" Then he waves the train on.

Every year, more than 750,000 passengers use what is probably the world's most unusual railroad and certainly one of the most unusual attractions on the Continent. Running for nearly seven miles, the Pioneer Railway of Budapest is staffed almost entirely by children ranging in age from eight to fourteen. The dream of every Hungarian boy—and quite a few girls, too—is to hit the cinder trail on the Pioneer Railway, learn the business of railroading by five or six years of actual experience and, one day (when grown up), move into a fulltime railroad job either at home or abroad.

Back in 1948, red-cheeked teenagers built the mountainside railroad themselves, with their own hands. Cutting roads into the limestone soil of Szechenyi Hill, which overlooks the silver band of the Danube River and gives a dilating panoramic view of the Hungarian metropolis, the small fry constructed the railway in less than a year's time.

Tourists who visit Budapest inevitably hear of the children's railroad and inevitably think it is a toy of some kind, or a Luna Park type of ride for kids from six to sixty. Quite the contrary. The railroad is a real, full-sized railroad. And most of the people who travel on it, primarily to get from one place to another and not for fun or diversion, are adults. Nor is there anything diminutive about the cars, the stations or the equipment. The only small things are the personnel. And they do their work in a big way. The boys and girls handle everything. They manage the stations, sell the tickets, superintend the control towers, handle the telegraph apparatus and even supervise the snack bars at each of the six stations and the two depots. Under the watchful eye of a grown-up teacher, they also drive the diesel engines and take care of maintenance.

Apart from the functional aspects, the railroad is a picturesque affair—at least, the stations are—considering the territory the line covers. The Elore station, for example, is nestled among ancient beech trees and, because of a nearby ski jump, it handles an enormous traffic during the winter. The Normafa station, on the other hand, is on the site of an old giant beech under which, for over a hundred years, Budapest staged open-air performances of Bellini's opera, "Norma," a special favorite in Hungary.

No railroad would be complete without a tunnel and the Pioneer Railway has a dandy one as you approach the Harshegy station which is around a bend. Built for practical and technical reasons, the tunnel runs 656 feet through a hillside of bewitching beauty. At the Csilleberc station, where a cozy railroad museum has been set up, the 250 Lilliputian trainmen are quartered in caboose-like barracks. Nightly you can hear the choo-children singing the Magyar version of "I've Been Working on the Railroad" with the kind of gusto that comes from trainees whose future is bright and who know that they are on the right track.

THE "GIRL MARKET"

LOOKING FOR A WIFE? Come to the once-a-year "Girl Market" of Gaina and pick one out. This is the way many men who worked in the far spread mountains of Transylvania did it for years and years before the Red regime put some brakes on one of the most unusual folkways in Europe.

Once every year the outdoor "Girl Market" stages its annual event which is now officially more of a folklore tourist attraction. But let's call a spade a spade and say that, in spite of Communist authorities who say "No! No!," a peasant lass will say "Yes! Yes!" if she likes the young feller who asks for her hand. After all, this is how mountain women of Transylvania have been finding husbands for centuries and no Johnny-come-lately government is going to tell these hardy females how to land a man. Today, therefore, the yearly occurrence—which usually takes place on the next to the last Sunday in July—is carried out in such a way that the Romanian secret police (many of whom deliberately look the other way) do not notice it if a would-be husband shopping for a mate proposes to a girl "on sale in the market." Oh, there are other attractions like folk dancing exhibitions, comedy skits, games of skill and chance, gastronomic tidbits and souvenirs to buy aplenty. But the some fifty thousand people who visit Gaina Mountain in Romania on that particular Sunday all keep their nosey eyes focused for the open-air marriage negotiations, deals that are often closed in a matter of seconds.

How did Gaina come about? Centuries ago someone had a bright idea, no doubt a woman. Because the men of Transylvania would leave home to work at their solitary jobs as shepherds for six months at a time before taking a week's vacation, the girls who stayed behind had little chance to meet eligible males their age. And so it was decided that, on one day of the year, the men from all over the scattered hills could convene at a designated spot and so would the gals. Selected as the meeting place was Gaina Mountain, a few hours drive from the city of Cluj.

Hundreds of beauties deeming themselves ready for marriage would dress up in their best finery, pack all their personal belongings and the livestock that poppa offered them and display all this and themselves at Gaina's "Girl Market"—where all parties went to reach a fancy figure. During the day, the boys would parade up and down and size up Cupid's candidates before making a pick. Any girl who agreed right on the spot to become some man's wife would close up her trunks and valises and go off with her newfound husband to live wherever he happened to have his home. Mother and Dad would be there to beam approval. According to some unofficial records, nearly every maiden who marketed herself at Gaina ended up married. Once wed, the new husband went off again to the faraway hills with his sheep—to come home only periodically. Communication between him and his wife was kept up with an ancient system of blowing on long, ten-foot horns. The women would blow these elongated trumpets using a code language and hubby would always have news from back

Hopeful mother
arranges her daughter's dresses
at annual Gaina "Girl Market"
(PHOTO COURTESY
ROMANIAN TOURIST AGENCY).

home. Let there be a note signalling danger and in a matter of minutes the lone spouse would have enough help on hand until her absentee husband reached the scene.

When the Communists came into power, they put their collective foot down. No more marriage mart, they ordered. Instead they set up Gaina as a tourist event, a festival of folkloristic entertainment, and in the beginning most of the girls were afraid to put themselves on the block. A few who broke the new rule got stiff jail sentences but, after a while, a certain laxity crept in and, before long, the "Girl Market" was once again going about its

sweet business. The *modus operandi,* however, is less obvious.

Though the Communist regime has not been able to curb the "Market," the women who run the Gaina impose but a single regulation on every transaction: Only one to a customer!

Footpath in Postumia Cave (PHOTO COURTESY JUGOTOURIST/BELGRADE).

HERE IN THIS SIDE POCKET of Slovenia, halfway between Trieste and Ljubljana, you can embark on a voyage to the center of the earth. Nature fashioned in the bowels of Yugoslavia an underworld of petrified primeval forest whose weirdness, it is claimed, inspired Dante when he wrote his *Inferno*. The cave of Postumia stuns each and every visitor once he has crossed its threshold and wended his way through a labyrinth of *Alice in Wonderland* pathways which have a fascinating echo, echo, echo . . .

Notable for its black-stained walls, the vestibule to the Postumia grotto was ravaged by a tremendous fire in 1944. A

A SUBTERRANEAN MAZE

Yugoslav guerrilla sneaked through the full length of the cave from another entrance and set fire to a Nazi gasoline and ammo dump that burned for a week. The roof and sides will remain black as an eternal memorial of the heroic struggle of the Slovene people against Hitler's army of occupation.

You do the first few miles of your shivery, thirteen–mile tour of this subterranean maze (average temperature 47°F.) chugging aboard a peewee railroad that runs on a big storage battery. Later you meander on foot through semi-illuminated tunnels of sights incomparable. It is a sensation you retain forever as you edge perilously deeper into a down-under stone jungle Ripley would not have believed. Mysterious rushing rivers suddenly appear out of nowhere and vanish into nowhere. With its magic wand of crystalline stalagmites and stalactites, Nature reveals to you innumerable stone-like humans and beasts of every description, spectacular medieval castles with palm trees, mighty obelisks and fantastically shaped cascading fountains. But then, from time to time, you are awakened in this frozen fairyland by the reality of an ice-cold droplet of water mischievously plunking down on you from a crack overhead.

One of the live unforgettable sights beneath the Yugo top crust is a species of Ice Age fish which swims around oblivious to the fact that it has no eyes. The peculiar creature (*Proteus anguineus*), known as "man-fish" here, has no corresponding relative anywhere in the present fauna world. This survivor from seventy million years ago, provided with both lungs and gills, has an unusual way of procreating. Sometimes it will produce its young from eggs and other times the young are born alive from its body, depending on the temperature of the cave water. Close up, you can ogle these eyeless creatures to your heart's content in special fish tanks as you stand on the Iron Bridge overlooking the Pivka River that disappears like a silver ribbon into a spooky cavern.

Another sight that challenges human imagination is "The Great Mountain" (157 feet high), the largest known underground mountain in the world. Nearby is the "Tunnel of Names," the walls of which are full of old signatures that go back to the early thirteenth century.

Created by centuries of the seeping water's ceaseless activity, the fantasy forms inside the Postumia cave defy description. The guides have given names to these creations. Among the most striking are "The Sleeping Lion," "The Great Waterfall," "The Sea Crab," "The Turkish Pipe," "The Lighthouse," "The Parrot," "The Melon" and "Sophia Loren." The last photogenic stalagmite has the same measurements as Sophia's monumental exterior.

By and by, as you continue through the eternal nirvana, you reach "The Concert Hall," an enormous salon that covers more than 32,000 square feet and can accommodate 10,000 people. Dances, wedding receptions and concerts are often held in this gigantic chamber. During the tourist season, from April 1 until October 30, there is a post office open here, with the only underground mailbox to be found anywhere. Eventually you come to the greatest treasure of Yugoslavia's cellar of surprises, "The Mighty Curtain." This is a delicately rainbow-hued stalactite three eighths of an inch thick with the shape and folds of a real hanging curtain. When Napoleon marched his French troops through the town of Postumia, he made a personal stop in the subterranean vale and later remarked that "The Mighty Curtain" was the most incredible sight he had ever seen.

Indeed overwhelmed, Napoleon asked: "Can such things be?"

You will certainly pose the same question when you come here and do your own exploration of this Yugo grotto which at one time belonged to Italy. Yes, Postumia can be described as nothing short of tour-ific!

WAYSIDE STONE MEMORIALS

THEY STAND BY THE WAYSIDE, dozens and dozens of them, silent but eloquent. Tourists pass them by, dozens and dozens of times, but rarely stop to pause and reflect about them. Yet Yugoslavia's wayside funeral monuments constitute one of the most unusual authentic travel sights to be found in Europe.

Death is not looked upon by the Serbians the way it is by other people. There is a curious reconciliation with it, which is brought out in the roadside stone memorials a traveler will see from time to time as he moves in and around Belgrade. These *"krajputasi"* (which means "by the road") invariably mark the spot where a person died or was killed. On some of the wayside stones, which can also mark a grave, the whole history of the deceased person is often portrayed without words. This is done through pictures of the objects which played an important part in his life or her life—a sewing machine, a scissors, a knife, a deck of cards, a hoe, a bottle of wine with a glass, a rifle, a book, a medal, a lathe, peasant sandals. . . .

Dating from the beginning of the nineteenth century, when the odd custom began, the strange rectangles have inscriptions on them to give the passer-by a wink, a cheerful word, or something to ponder. Here is an example: "We are born to die, but we die to live eternally!"

A few miles away, you will read this thought on another stone:

"I was like you, and you will be like me. . . ."

Adorned with figures of beautiful women, rapturous boys gazing up at heaven, mothers with outstretched arms, soldiers with their medals and rifles at their sides, the monuments have a special pull for attracting Yugoslavs and getting them to take a few moments of rest. It is not uncommon to see a family of natives, unrelated to the deceased, having a picnic on a memorial site and sharing what they are eating and drinking with the departed one by pouring some wine, for instance, onto the grass.

Each roadside monument is unique in its own way. There is one just outside Belgrade which shows a young man with a fez in the company of a village beauty. The text reads: "Now he is alone in his earth. You who read this cannot come near him even in thought. He knows what you do not and what you will never discover until you cross into his world."

The curious memorials to the dead, mind you, are never found in cemeteries, as you would expect, but only along roads. Oxcarts, automobiles, bicycles, tractors, foot travelers—they are the ones for whom the "billboards" are intended. The carved-in-stone words exhort such passers-by with: "Stop a while, brother, take your time! Sit on the grass and rest a little—and read these sad words. Speak the name of a Serbian soldier."

Rain over the years has washed the face of hundreds of these stones, dimmed the eyes, faded the colors and worn down the words. Often high weeds have grown around the silent markers or in some cases they have begun to sink or lean. But, no matter. The natives still take time to pause, rest and meditate in their presence.

Occasionally the inscriptions report miniature legends, as witness:

"Beneath this marble slab rest the earthly remains of Gajo Bugarcic, headman of the village of Lipnica for fifteen years, to the satisfaction of all. He was well-known for his sound judgment. On March 1st, 1863, he was shot by a thief through the window of his house and in the space of three hours entered eternal life in his fifty-second year. His death was a bitter blow. But it brought relief through the stricter enforcement of law, so that thieves were exterminated, whereas be-fore his death, honest people enjoyed no safety of person or property. O, good man, may the black earth lie lightly on the powder of your bones."

Near the small town of Valjevo stands a tilted *krajputasi* which is a favorite with the locals. The stone marks the very spot where a soldier fell in battle against the Turks in 1814. Intended for a chuckle, the message reads: "I lie here and you read, but it would be better if you were lying and I were reading."

Picnic at wayside memorial stones
(PHOTO COURTESY OF JUGOTOURIST/BELGRADE).

*Monoklissia women celebrating
at the Christos Lentas Inn
on their one day of the year.*

"LADIES' DAY"
IN GREECE

ONCE A YEAR, usually during the second week of January, this tiny Thracian village stages "Ladies' Day," when the men and women switch roles for a full twenty-four hours. There is nothing like it for any tourist who happens to wander by on this ancient festival day—which really is not a "festival" in the usual sense of the word. But all male travelers are herewith warned not to show face in Monoklissia on "Ladies' Day" because gangs of women will apprehend him, drag him to the main square and douse him with water.

This is the day, with some ancient hard and fast rules prevailing, when at dawn all males are confined to the house or farm, there to cope with the kids, wash and dry the dishes, milk the cows, prepare the meals and do all the cleaning. The Women's Lib people should look into this ere long. . . .

Meanwhile, the wives do what most of the town Toms do for the other 364 days of the year. They congregate at the cafe, gamble at cards, recount boastful stories about themselves, tell a few off-color anecdotes and comport themselves rowdily. It is the day when non-smokers smoke, non-drinkers drink and non-gamblers gamble.

During "Ladies' Day," the only men allowed on the streets are the parish priest and a hired bagpiper. The latter is blindfolded and his job is to play in the square all day long (with time out for one meal) while the women whoop it up with folk dances, some of which are quite suggestive. Any man who ventures on the street pays the penalty of an ignominious cold-water drenching, brrr. . . . By nightfall, the bagpiper, still blindfolded, is so low in spirits he cannot hit his high notes any more, but he dare not quit. The Christos Lentas inn rings with bawdy songs (for soprano voice) while prodigious quantities of wine are washed down to whet wifey's whistle. Highlight of the evening is a big dinner served at the Christos Len-

150

tas. The bill of fare includes roast rooster (never hen or duck) and a selection of fruits and vegetables, usually bananas and cucumbers. As dawn approaches, the party breaks up and jolly Molly wends her way home. Momma usually makes hubby serve up a cup of coffee as her last shot before the sun rises to signal the end of "Ladies' Day."

Monoklissia's one day of gynecocratic rule is a survival of ancient fertility rites which go back several centuries and which most likely had as their foundation the stimulus of the theme of Aristophanes' play, *Lysistrata*, in which the women go on strike against their husbands. This explanation, though advanced by anthropologists at Athens University, is scoffed at by people who prefer to believe that Monoklissia was once the seat of the original Amazon matriarchy in which the Queen maintained a harem of fifteen men and all her warriors had smaller harems of seven men each.

"This is the day," explains Ileana Arghyris, a housewife who lives in a red-tiled cottage on the dirt road leading to the Bulgarian border, "that we make the men suffer. For twenty-four hours we get even with the male sex. We hand over our aprons and our dishcloth—and heaven help him who goes against the rules while it's our turn to hold the upper hand."

Mrs. Arghyris explains this shortly before she and some of her comrades reel off under the influence of wine to serenade under some former beau's window. One sad policeman whose wife takes over his morning duty as the

town traffic cop watches this through his window and offers this complaint: "I don't mind staying home one day of the year doing all the housework, even though I have four young children to take care of. It's a wonder how I ever manage to see the day through. But the least my wife could do is to make the beds before she leaves."

On "Ladies' Day," Monoklissia abounds in husbandly fumbles and grumbles, for whatever else may be said about the males in this town, they do not quite like it when wifey indulges in her annual she-nanigans.

Monoklissia man remains at home and does the usual household chores (PHOTOS BY RAPHAELIDIS OF ATHENS).

THE LAND OF NO WOMEN

NEXT TO MILITARY GOODS and petroleum, the biggest business in the world is tourism, but you'd never suspect it here in the Holy Athonite Republic because half of the possible tourist population is barred by laws that go back to the year 1060 A.D. and are still strictly enforced. No women are allowed!

Yes, the geography of this country, perhaps the only theocracy in the world and the only monastic state in Europe, remains undefiled by the presence of members of the opposite sex. "No Women's Land," nevertheless, is a tourist attraction that does not encourage tourism but, if you are of the male persuasion, and are willing to put up with a lot of inconvenience, Mount Athos will let you come in for a look-see.

But you can't bring along a wife, or girl friend, or mistress, or Susie Q. or even a pet dog, cat or parakeet that happens to be female. *She* is a no no, a nix, forbidden, *verboten*, no way! Those are the rigid rules kept by the

Several of the monks at Mount Athos
(PHOTO BY JIMMY BEDFORD).

nine hundred monks of Mount Athos. So if you are female, you can only read this chapter because a trip to Mount Athos is for men only.

With a status somewhat akin to that of Vatican City, Mount Athos is plopped on a mountainous peninsula nearly forty miles long and four miles wide, jutting into the Aegean Sea some 150 miles east of Salonika. The sanctuary of barricaded bachelors who inhabit this almost inaccessible country is one of the curiosities of human history and promises to be the last male stronghold on the planet.

Extending from the coast of Greece and rising 6,350 feet above sea level, Athos is independent of Greek jurisdiction and is governed by monastic orders of the Greek Orthodox Church. The monks who live, work and pray here in the twenty monasteries in twelve "towns" have no radio, no television, no newspapers, no telephones and only one vehicle. Besides the restrictions on milady, they also have severe laws against all musical instruments, smoking, horseback riding, transistor radios, cassette players and singing.

If you are visiting on foot or by pack mule, the land where time stood still offers you one monastery after another. What I found in these places were immaculate sleeping quarters, substantial vegetarian food with plenty of fresh water or wine and no-problem plumbing. The Vatopedi Monastery, which smells like the winery it is, runs the closest thing to a hotel. Meals, which are eaten in silence, consist of lentil soup, fish, salad and home baked bread, plus wine or water. What is refreshing indeed is that no one will ever ask for money or even suggest a payment, but tipping is not discouraged.

Male tourists have to go to the trouble of getting a special permit through the Greek Ministry of Foreign Affairs in Athens or the Ministry of Northern Greece in Salonika, plus a card that costs about four dollars and is called "diamonitirion" from the Athos governmental agent, entitling you to free room and board. Your entry into Athos is through the port of Dafni which you reach by a coastal boat from the town of Ouranoupolis.

For the female tourist who may be intrigued by a place like the Holy Mountain, one way to see it, without fuss or bother, is to rent a motor launch or take an organized Aegean Sea junket from Piraeus to ogle Adam's Seventh Heaven through glasses.

The gentlemen's utopia rises above the lazy brine of the Aegean like an overgrown pyramid to a steep summit of white marble. Along the flanks of the mountain are the monastic villages, the first of which was established in 274 A.D. Each of the monasteries is built with massive stone walls and has watchtowers with slit windows, buildings giving the impression of being able to hold out against heavy aerial bombardments.

At St. Denis Monastery, you will find a priceless collection of rare Byzantine documents, precious icons, the preserved hand of John the Baptist and a splinter from the cross of Christ which is the monastery's most cherished object. Since all the monks are scholars, quite a few of them speak book-English and are eager to practice it.

When questioned about the no-female rules, one longbeard said from a happy, ruddy-olive face that was one of the healthiest mine eyes have seen: "The life here is good. It is quiet. And it is rewarding. We live longer in Athos than people do anywhere else in the world. Why do we need women here? It took one woman to undo the Garden of Eden. It will take the same number to damn Athos."

153

THE FIRE WALKERS OF MACEDONIA

EVER SINCE THE END of World War II, when the strange religious rite of the Anastenaria began to be performed in public, biologists and anthropologists have been taking an interest in the soles of the feet of the fire walkers of Macedonia in Northeastern Greece. It is now an established fact that, no matter how long the frenzied dancers prance on the live charcoal embers, their bare feet remain unscathed. What is even more incredible is that the little hairs on their toes do not even get singed.

Every year in the village of Langada, thirteen miles from Salonika, members of the ancient Anastenaria cult perform their weird dances on May 21. If you happen to be visiting either Langada, Ayia Eleni, Mavrolefki or Meliki when the ceremonies are to take place and, if you can stand the spine-chilling shrieks that rend the air, then you are due for what may well be one of the most overwhelming experiences of your life. The dancers skip and jump and hop among the glowing coals with their tootsies bared. Nevertheless, a skeptical onlooker, suspecting some kind of fakery, is welcome to touch what he wants and see for himself if it is at all phony. University professors who have given minute examination to all phases of the fire walking ritual still have not been able to explain just why the participants never get burned.

A few years ago one team of psychologists from the University of Athens, having watched the eye-arresting performance here in Langada, offered this theoretical explanation: "The state of frenzy, which the fire-walking entertainers induce, brings on psychic waves from the body, these act as an insulating screen from any fire, however real."

Originally the mysterious and centuries-steeped Anastenaria inhabited the village of Kosti in Eastern Thrace, Bulgaria. The cult began a thousand years or so ago when fire swept through Kosti's church one night and the townfolk heard their ikons moaning and groaning. Some of the villagers bravely rushed into the blazing church to carry eight relics to safety. Incredibly, those who did emerged from the inferno with no blisters or burns on their feet, though they had to scamper across wooden floors that were aflame.

During the exchange of populations between Greece and Bulgaria in 1914, the Kosti inhabitants were resettled in the four towns in that part of Macedonia belonging to Greece and they brought with them their eight ikons, to which they attribute occult powers. Now each year on the anniversary of the fire the descendants of the ikon-savers repeat their ancestors' feat, protected by the original holy relics which they hold during their fire dance.

Because the Greek Orthodox Church did not endorse the Anastenaria cult and the fire dancing, it forced the annual feast to go underground for centuries. But, today, instead of being performed on the q.t., the dance is carried out before the eyes of the public. Giant sightseeing buses from Salonika and other cities come in all day long and a camp chair around the central square becomes a precious thing as shish kebab sellers, peanut

154

vendors and barefoot boys hawking fans lend a hubbub air of excitement to the upcoming evening event. During the afternoon a huge log fire is lit and, by nightfall, the logs have burned down to a bed of coals that are several inches deep and cover an area of about ten square yards. Then the fire dancers, most of whom are men, appear on the scene, do a bit of jogging around the pit (like an athlete warming up for a track meet) and then, one by one, as the crowd hushes, jump onto the red-hot coals for some brief but spirited hopping.

As the Anastenaria men and women go through their sizzling paces, you know you are seeing an event that will never miss fire—the hottest show in town.

Frenzied dancers prance
on live charcoal embers at Langada
(PHOTO BY RAPHAELIDIS OF ATHENS).

THE TOURISTS' KREMLIN

HOWEVER OMINOUS "Kremlin" sounds to a foreigner's ears and forbidding to his eyes, as he views the towers of Communism standing stern guard over Red Square, it invariably comes as a sheer surprise to all visitors here that they are perfectly free to go behind the Kremlin's portentous walls for a tour of the grounds and a visit into the buildings. Though the Kremlin, which has seen history aplenty since it was built in 1491, is the seat of the Soviet government, it is also one of Moscow's biggest tourist attractions. A visitor entering the grounds does not pay any admission fee nor does he undergo restrictions as he wanders below the conelike spires and onion domes that have known both Tsars and Stalin.

As a witness to Russia's revolutionary history and as headquarters for Soviet power, the Kremlin is rarely thought of as a monument—which is what it is. In actual fact, the word *"kremlin"* means citadel. And to give you an idea of how impenetrable a fortress it is, suffice to say that the mile and a half of walls that surround this political nerve center are three to seven yards thick and often stand as high as sixty-two feet.

Once inside the Kremlin walls, the tourist gets his next biggest surprise: there are three dreamlike church structures that grace the main square. The five-domed Uspensky Cathedral, completed in 1479, houses famous frescoes and the carved walnut throne of Ivan the Terrible. In the Archangelsky Cathedral, which was finished in 1509, are buried most of the early Tsars, including Ivan the Terrible and the son

he murdered. The Annunciation Cathedral with its nine domes displays the most precious ikons in Russia. Opposite the three cathedrals is a building that will likely sponge up hours of your time if you are interested in such things as Boris Godunov's throne, jewel-encrusted carriages, the boots of Peter the Great (which give an idea of just how big this seven-foot monarch really was), a church garment whose pearls alone weigh over thirty pounds and the ancient Cap of Monomakh with which Ivan III crowned his grandson Dmitri.

One place the police will not let you visit, however, is the Grand Kremlin Palace, built in 1849. This not only has the private apartments and offices used by figures like Lenin, Stalin, Khrushchev and the current bosses but also houses the chambers where the U.S.S.R. parliament holds its sessions.

Perhaps one of the most interesting structures within the Kremlin is the showcase modernistic Palace of Congresses, which the Soviets insist on calling the world's greatest theatre building. And well it may be. In addition to operas and ballets (the Bolshoi Ballet puts on grandiose performances there), the Palace of Congresses is used by the Communist Party for its mass meetings and international conferences. Erected in 1961, the building has a stupendous white marble glassed-in vestibule with ivory-colored escalators leading to various levels of the spacious auditorium seating six thousand. Above the main auditorium is a second one, seating 2,500, which is set on steel springs and which is often used for state dinners, receptions, balls and gala parties.

Broken bell in the Kremlin.

The most curious of all the behind the Kremlin walls attractions and certainly the most photographed is the largest bell in Russia, which the citizenry calls the "king of bells." Cast in 1735, it has never once rung because it fell from its scaffolding while being installed and a chip weighing a mere twelve tons broke off. Today the bell stands on a low pedestal in the Kremlin's main square as film fodder.

Near the broken bell is the "king of cannons," weighing forty tons. Cast in 1586 and intended for the Tartar invasions, the gun was supposed to fire two ton cannon balls a half mile or so but, like the nearby bell, it never even made a sound. In the old days folks used to say: "Tsar Bell doesn't ring, Tsar Cannon doesn't fire and Tsar Nicholas doesn't reign!"

With five gates serving an enclosed area of sixty-four acres, the Kremlin is a touristic "must" with its architectural battlements and dialectical materialism, its ancient stones and hard heads.

157

THE
MOSCOW SUBWAY

EXTENDING A LONG bear hug to tourists, the Russian capital wants to get travelers to come to Soviet soil—but one of the most intriguing attractions here is not on Soviet ground but underneath it. All politics aside, a visitor to Moscow should go underground and explore the Moscow subway.

The "Metro" (to give it its Paris-originated Russian name) carries the highest density of riders (3,500,000 a day) of any subway or railroad in the world. But this is not what makes the Moscow subway the architectural underground wonder that it is. Muscovites are proud of their subterranean choo-choo and actively encourage tourists—sometimes even taking them by the hand—to descend for a look-see.

Once down below, after having paid the five kopecks fare (six cents), the tourist finds himself visiting different stations that look like tunneled-out palaces. With hanging crystal chandeliers and stairways and platforms made of granite, marble and even semiprecious stones, each train stop is a site to see. Some of the stations have walls fitted with murals and frescoes, stained glass, artful floodlighting, molded stucco and other florid, grandiose features. There are statues and paintings galore by Russia's top artists and some of the barrel-vaulted ceilings are covered with mosaics such as you only see in Italian churches. And let's not even mention the many-colored marble columns and rows and rows of eight-sided pylons which abound from station to station.

From an architectural point of view, perhaps the most striking station is the Kropotkinskaya station, which was built by the U.S.S.R.'s two most important architects, Dushkin and Likhtenberg, who, allotted an equal share of space down below, were given a free hand to outdo one another. The result is a hodge of ornate splendor and a podge of stylistic designs that could give a rubbernecking art critic a case of my-oh-myopia. Because there are almost 250 miles of track and some seventy stations in the Metro with new stops being added every year, the tourist would want to hit the more interesting platforms, of course. Knowledgeable Muscovites, who have explored every nook of the underground webwork, say that one needs only an hour and a half.

By entering the Prospekt Marxa station, whose entrance is close to the Moskva Hotel in the very heart of the city, the tourist would first stop at the Kropotkinskaya. Then he should take a train going in the same direction for pauses at the Park Kultury station and the Leninskiye station. At this point he should cross the platform and take a train going back to Park Kultury where he transfers to a train which will take him to the Oktyabrskaya and Dobryninskaya stations. By making a few other transfers, the tourist who wants more of this optical profusion ought to visit Komsomolskaya, Mayakovskaya, Kievskaya, Bylelorusskaya and Ploschchad Sverdlova stations, at which point he can exit and find himself back once again downtown at Revolution Square.

Getting around the subway, despite language problems, is easy. To find out how to get where, use one of the electric maps at each station, press the button with the name of your stop and the lighted stretch of track will show you the quickest route. Or do what my wife and I did—we simply copied the station name down in the Cyrillic letters which we did not understand and showed them to any passenger. With Russian hospitality, many led us personally (often by taking our hands, as if we were children) to the track.

The trains, which travel at a speed of sixty miles an hour, come every ninety seconds and are driverless, though a man does sit in the cab just to make sure the automatic pilot functions. A powerful ventilation system changes the air seven times an hour and, according to chief operation engineer Igor Fyalkovsky, "you breathe purer air underground than you do at street level."

One word of warning: Just don't do the Moscow subway during the crush hour because like anywhere else in the world the people are too busy russian home.

*Two stations
in the Moscow subway*
(PHOTO COURTESY INTOURIST).

BIRD MARKET
IN MOSCOW

MORE THAN JUST BIRDS of a feather flock together at Moscow's unique "Bird Market," a tourist attraction not listed in your guidebook to Russia. During the warm months the ornithological carnival holds sway on Sundays between six a.m. and three p.m. off the big Kalitnikovskaya Street and no visitor in Moscow should miss it for the world.

As one of the very few free enterprise activities allowed in the Soviet Union, the weekly market draws thousands of pet lovers and other thousands just to watch and amble among the rows of birdcages, fish tanks, reptile jars, rabbit crates, kitten cartons and paper sacks full of turtles, toads and take-your-pick.

In Chekhov's day, the bird market used to offer animal fanciers their

160

choice of hedgehogs, skylarks, chipmunks—just about everything except a sperm whale or a dodo. Chekhov, fascinated by the bustling mart, wrote a short story about it in 1883, when it was located at Tube Square, in which he said: "It lives its own life. It twirls and bustles and to those business-minded and church-bound people, what is this bizarre collection of workmen's hats and peasant caps and society people's stovepipes, what are all those characters jabbering about and bargaining over?"

Since then the century-old bird market has moved its location several times. Today for a twenty-kopeck payment (approximately twenty-four cents), any Soviet citizen can put pets up for sale. But they do not necessarily have to be pets. One Russian farmer comes in every week with a dozen rabbits he has caught in his fields and peddles the cottontails at about a dollar per. Nobody has ever bothered to ascertain whether these members of Rodentia are kept as household companions or used to grace a dinner table for company.

True lovers of tropical fish, many Muscovites belong to clubs which devote a lot of time to cultivating new species. The vendors of rare fish breeds do a good business with the home aquarium crowd. "Look at this ichthyological marvel!" shouts one bespectacled barker holding up a jar with a transparent, bluish fellow swimming around in all his eighth-of-an-inch glory.

Over on the other side are the songbirds. They are to be found in arcades and in cages hung by nails to fences in the shady part. Though there are pigeon lovers galore, much interest is always centered around those cages where the vendor has bred cursing parrots or canaries whose feathers resemble a movie rainbow. On sale also is a sad-faced nightingale but the price is stiff and nobody wants to invest that much, even if the creature does have a "please buy me" look on his face week in and week out.

Curiously enough, puppies and kittens do not sell well in Moscow. The reason for this is that dogs and cats eat meat and meat is not always plentiful in the Soviet Union. Besides, with all apartments overcrowded and hardly any space left for people, furry quadrupeds would only get in the way. Almost the only Russians who buy canines and felines are farm people who live away from the city.

Though all the sellers compete in loud voices, it is not unusual to see less aggressive salesmen sitting against a box napping. Their wares—whether denizens of the sea or critters of the ozone—are in jars or cages tied to leather thongs around their necks. At Moscow's misnamed "Bird Market" you are bound to meet all animal types—except perhaps a scapegoat, a lame duck, a sacred cow or an acrobat.

But the biggest sellers are the birds—hence the name. A lot of birds get sold here during the traditional "bird week" when all good boys and girls consider it their privilege "to free at least one bird." So one is usually bought out of little Boris' savings and then, later that day, amid ceremonial fuss from members of the immediate family, one proud tyke liberates the feathered prisoner, usually a pigeon.

And off he goes, winging his way back to the coop of the vendor who originally put him up for sale at the picturesque bird market of Moscow.

161

"INGLISH" BEHIND THE IRON CURTAIN

NOW THAT THE Communist nations have opened their doors to set out welcome mats for American tourists who bring in those lovable dollar bills, the Reds are putting spit and polish to their English at the expense of the English language. What was once therefore the "war of words" between us and them has now become a "war on words" between them and us.

Hotels and elevators constitute the soft underbelly of Communism. It seems the Marxists are having words with the King's "Inglish," as witness the samples of skewed syntax this writer has accumulated during his travels behind the Iron Curtain.

In Belgrade's state-owned skyscraper hotel, the Slavija, the elevator instructions tell users: "1. To move the cabin push button of wishing floor. 2. If the cabin should enter more persons, each one should press number of wishing floor. Driving is then going alphabetically by natural order. 3. Button retaining pressed position shows received command for visiting station."

Posted on the door of my room in the same hotel was this notice: "Let Us Know About Any Unficiency As Well As Leaking On The Service. Our Utmost Will Improve It."

Not to be outdone by anybody in this dialect materialism, the Hungarians once handed out printed folders to visiting athletes during an international sporting event which said: "Sports in the rotting capitalistic countries are the declared enemy of the Socialist athletes who consider it their duty to worth the superiority of the Socialist races. Yet we wish you good luck. Our applause for

you will be as enthusiastic, but mind that this applause is never delivered to the capitalistic system, of which we have our own views."

As if that were not enough for the Magyars, in many of their plush hotel rooms you are likely to read the warning: "All rooms not denounced by twelve o'clock will be paid for twicely."

While aboard a Soviet ship in the Black Sea, I found the following lifesaving instructions on my cabin door: "Helpsavering apparata in emergings behold many whistles! Associate the stringing apparata about the bosoms and meet behind. Flee then to the indifferent lifesavering shippen obediencing the instructs of the vessel chef." The Russians are also proud of their ice cream, a type which one of their ambassadors to Washington brought from the United States and which Soviet dieticians copied quite successfully. On the wrapper of a gummy but yummy cone, one is privileged to be told: "Do not taste our Ice Cream when it is too hard. Please continue your conversation until the Ice Cream grows into a softer. By adhering this advisement you will fully appreciate the wonderful Soviet Ice Cream."

On a highway in Poland there is a sign that tells foreign motorists to "Go soothingly in the snow, as there lurk the ski demons." Another Polish traffic sign: "Right Turn Toward Immediate Outside."

Strolling in the heart of downtown Warsaw, you can buy "U.S. Ham Burgers" and for the Britons there is even a cafe which serves "Five O'Clock Tea At All Hours." The theatre program issued

Sign on a hotel elevator in Bucharest.

THE LIFT IS
BEING FIXED
FOR THE NEXT
DAYS. DURING
THAT TIME
WE REGRET THAT
YOU WILL BE
UNBEARABLE

during a performance of "Rigoletto" in Warsaw's spanking-new opera house says that "the act ends with the rape of Gilda, organized by the knight Marullo, which is convinced doing so, to play a vindictive joke to the buffoon of whom the young lady is considered lover."

In Prague a stateside traveler also gets the impression the Czechs have never bothered to double-Czech mangling participles. For example, take this questionable piece of prose in the office of Cedok, Czechoslovakia's state tourist agency: "Take One Of Our Horse-Driven City Tours—We Guarantee No Miscarriages."

But of all the tricky translations I have collected in the Communist World, perhaps this one deserves a special plaque. I saw it on the elevator door of a Bucharest hotel lobby: "The lift is being fixed for the next days. During that time we regret that you will be unbearable."

163

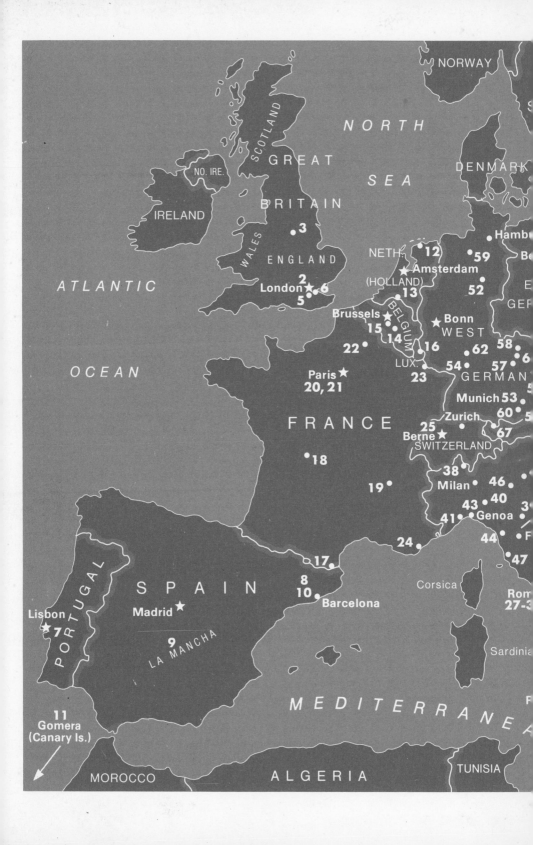